Dear Reader:

The book you are about to 1[...] Martin's True Crime Library, the imprint *The New York Times* calls "the leader in true crime!" Each month, we offer you a fascinating account of the latest, most sensational crime that has captured the national attention. St. Martin's is the publisher of Tina Dirmann's VANISHED AT SEA, the story of a former child actor who posed as a yacht buyer in order to lure an older couple out to sea, then robbed them and threw them overboard to their deaths. John Glatt's riveting and horrifying SECRETS IN THE CELLAR shines a light on the man who shocked the world when it was revealed that he had kept his daughter locked in his hidden basement for 24 years. In the Edgar-nominated WRITTEN IN BLOOD, Diane Fanning looks at Michael Petersen, a Marine-turned-novelist found guilty of beating his wife to death and pushing her down the stairs of their home—only to reveal another similar death from his past. In the book you now hold, CRUEL HEART, William Van Meter examines a terrible crime on a Kentucky college campus.

St. Martin's True Crime Library gives you the stories behind the headlines. Our authors take you right to the scene of the crime and into the minds of the most notorious murderers to show you what really makes them tick. St. Martin's True Crime Library paperbacks are better than the most terrifying thriller, because it's all true! The next time you want a crackling good read, make sure it's got the St. Martin's True Crime Library logo on the spine—you'll be up all night!

Charles E. Spicer

Charles E. Spicer, Jr.
Executive Editor, St. Martin's True Crime Library

CRUEL HEART

A TRUE STORY OF MURDER IN KENTUCKY

William Van Meter

St. Martin's Paperbacks

Cruel Heart was previously published by Free Press under the title *Bluegrass*.

Lyrics from "The Party" by Chan Marshall reprinted by kind permission of Doorman/Mattitude Music LLC.

Published by arrangement with Free Press

CRUEL HEART

For information address Free Press, 1230 Avenue of the Americas, New York, NY 10020.

EAN: 978-0-312-37309-2

Printed in the United States of America

Free Press edition / January 2009
St. Martin's Paperbacks edition / December 2010

St. Martin's Paperbacks are published by St. Martin's Press, 175 Fifth Avenue, New York, NY 10010.

10 9 8 7 6 5 4 3 2 1

For Ferris Van Meter

Cruel Heart was composed from tape-recorded interviews, personal observation, and official records, such as police interrogations and court transcripts. All were edited for clarity and length. Unrecorded reconstructed conversations were derived from the recollections of one or more of the parties who partook or witnessed. Certain names have been changed.

Good friends comin' in
The party's about to begin
We can wrestle down to the floor
Throw empty bottles out the door

They will smash and we will laugh
What a gas we have had
The light from the window
Will cast our dancing shadows

Music from the back room
Is an old song
We all know
Through shining eyes and smiling faces
We all sing along

Been so long since I seen you
My good friends
This memory daydream
Is good enough for me

If you were here today
We'd be getting into frisky business
Maybe some other day
Dream
Memory

—Chan Marshall, "The Party"

PROLOGUE

May 4, 2003

The already unhurried pace of Bowling Green, Kentucky, had been slowing down to a crawl. The students at Western Kentucky University had only one more week of school before summer break. There were final exams and parties. But the tranquil start to the weekend would come to be remembered as the overture to a tragedy that would always be shrouded in mystery and confusion.

At 4:08 AM the fire alarm in Hugh Poland Hall went off. The ninety-decibel bleating awakened the slumbering residents, who filed down the stairs to exit.

Students in various states of undress were on the dorm lawn rubbing their bleary eyes. The grass was damp with morning dew and mist hung in the air. Spring was slowly shifting into summer and it was still chilly. Many were annoyed for having to wake up so early for what they thought was just another fire drill. Some girls were mortified to be seen in such a disheveled state and frantically tried to tame their wild, slept-on hair. Two boys ran after a giggling girl like puppies chasing a butterfly.

Suddenly everyone stopped moving. Silence swept over them like a great wave when the doors swung open and two firemen emerged carrying one of their classmates wrapped in a sheet and set her on the ground. She was nude save for the sheer wrap tied around her face and a T-shirt knotted around her neck. She was burnt black from her thighs all the way to her neck. A cadre of firemen surrounded her. They were a busy epicenter of noise and movement ringed by the quiet and stillness of the students, all played against the backdrop of the ceaselessly braying sirens and flashing red lights from the trucks.

I

CHAPTER 1

May 3, 2003

Although the sun was bright, the unrelenting summer heat had not yet arrived. It was nearing 2 PM in Scottsville, Kentucky, and Luke Goodrum was just getting up. Luke's routine was to wake up late, hang out with his girlfriend, Brittany, until she went on cashier duty at Food Lion, and then play video games until she was free. It was Derby Day, but Scottsville is about 100 miles and a world away from the Triple Crown race in Louisville.

Luke had stayed up late the night before playing video games and drinking beer with one of his high school buddies. He knew that he would have to go to Bowling Green, a much larger town twenty minutes northwest, with Brittany—in part to appease her for the night before when she had stopped by in the middle of a game. Luke had been extremely drunk and ignored her for the pixilated football players on the screen.

Luke showered and got ready, admiring himself in the mirror. He was twenty-one years old, six feet two inches tall, with dark blond hair and brown eyes. His 180-pound frame was cut from lifting weights. If he wasn't playing sports he was watching them. The amount of food he consumed was akin to a professional football player—he drank a gallon of milk each day by himself. Luke was garrulous, often smiling, and spoke in a heavily accented, rapid-fire drawl littered with double negatives and tenses out of whack. When Luke spoke, words burst out of his mouth with no spaces between them, a natural auctioneer. He had the air of a good ol' boy with a touch of hip-hop. A thin patch of a goatee sprouted below his lower lip; sideburns extended halfway past his earlobes. Luke was handsome and he knew it, and never had a problem with girls. In fact, Brittany had picked him up in the first place.

About eight months before, seventeen-year-old Brittany Stinson was cruising "the strip" in nearby Glasgow with a carload of girlfriends when she noticed Luke in the passenger seat of his friend's truck. Like many roads in so many small towns, "the strip" was a street gilded with fast-food franchises and telephone poles where the teenagers went on weekends. Brittany followed them into the McDonald's parking lot, leaned on the truck, and introduced herself. The following Monday, after school, Brittany went to Luke's apartment. They had been together ever since.

Luke liked being with someone as outgoing as he was, but he was admittedly more struck by her body. Brittany was about five feet five inches tall and petite. "Except for her butt," Luke pointed out to his buddies.

Luke folded a white bandanna with blue print and wrapped it around his forehead—it reminded him of both Axl Rose and Tupac Shakur. He phoned in a delivery order to Domino's and watched TV while eating the pepperoni pizza. Some of the garlic dipping sauce dribbled onto his T-shirt.

Although rather oblivious to it, Luke embodied a curious amalgam of each tier of Scottsville society. Currently out of work, Luke had held a litany of blue-collar jobs, such as house painter and truck stop attendant. None of his posts lasted long. Luke would either get fired, or more commonly, abruptly quit. He supplemented his wages by moonlighting, selling marijuana and, on occasion, cocaine.

Through his mother's second marriage, Luke was also connected to the richest and most well-known family in Scottsville, the Turners. Donna Dugas's second husband, Bruce Dugas, was a grandson of Cal Turner, the founder of the Dollar General store chain (essentially a less-discerning Kmart). The no-frills emporiums have shelves haphazardly stocked with a variety of discounted everyday items—loofahs, toothpaste, nails, clothing—just about anything imaginable. One of the first stores occupies a cornerstone of Scottsville's modest downtown square. Semitrucks emblazoned with the stark black on yellow DOLLAR GENERAL emblem on their trailers careen down the roads as they are dispatched from the giant warehouse on the outskirts of town. Despite the carefully cultivated small town image of the stores themselves, Dollar General is a Fortune 500 company with more than 7,600 outlets spread throughout the Southeast and $7.6 billion in annual sales. The latest in Luke's string of jobs had been loading trucks at the Dollar General warehouse. It wasn't a mystery how he got the job, nor was it surprising when he walked off and never came back.

In a tiny town like Scottsville, where everyone at least knows *of* one another even if they aren't direct acquaintances, the Turners' wealth became just another idiosyncrasy accepted by the community. Scottsville is a farm and factory town. Although the Turners' wealth wasn't a secret, it was not broadcast loudly. As a whole, the Turners weren't an ostentatious clan, and even resided in simple homes—far from the opulence possible. Scottsville was a unified community, so small that no one had a choice but to frequent the same shops and restaurants, no matter one's financial standing or race.

Bruce and Donna Dugas now lived on a sprawling horse ranch outside of Dallas, Texas.

On the other side of the financial spectrum was Luke's father, Mike Goodrum. Mike worked at the same engine parts factory as his third wife, Judy. They lived in a modest one-story home not far from Luke's apartment in Scottsville. Mike strove to instill a good work ethic in Luke but feared he was losing the battle.

As Luke was devouring his last slice of pizza, Brittany arrived at the apartment and joined him on the black futon. Her deeply bronzed skin made her bright green eyes stand out even more. She wore form-fitting jeans, a tight top that showed off her flat midriff, and sneakers.

The couple got into Brittany's car and headed off to Bowling Green. Brittany was driving her gray '93 Maxima with the seat as far back as it could go, her arm draped over the steering wheel like they do in rap videos. They took Brittany's car because Luke didn't want to take his treasured silver '96 Mustang.

He spent hours tinkering under the hood of that car. The Mustang's windows were impenetrably dark and the body was lowered so far it almost scraped the ground. The headlights were tinted blue and the hubcaps were mirrorlike chrome. The engine's roar sounded like a fighter jet because Luke had installed an H-pipe Flowmaster to the manifold. The bass booming from the speakers rattled windows when it drove past.

Luke had just gotten the clutch fixed and planned to sell the car. He hoped to get five thousand dollars for it to fund a move to Miami. Luke envisioned himself bartending in South Beach. He also thought about joining the air force. But all of Luke's future plans were vague, and moving to Miami was more a daydream than an actual goal. Luke had yet to pursue anything seriously. College was out of the question; academics were never a strong suit, and he had dropped out after a semester of community college. In fact, Luke had never read a book. He was equally uninterested in working.

Luke's ex-wife, LaDonna, was acutely aware of this—especially when she was expecting the monthly child support payment. LaDonna lived in nearby Franklin, Kentucky, with her and Luke's two-year-old son, Tyler. Luke and LaDonna dated during his senior year of high school and he got her pregnant just before graduating. Their relationship had been fiery and intense before it finally burnt out the year before. Their romance pulled all those around them into its strife and troubled passion, and LaDonna had filed multiple domestic violence petitions. A restraining order currently barred Luke from LaDonna, and he wasn't allowed to see Tyler without supervision. LaDonna was, in fact, engaged to marry the very next afternoon. This deeply bothered Luke and he couldn't get it out of his mind.

When not in Franklin with LaDonna or his maternal grandparents, Tyler often stayed with Luke's father. But lately, Luke avoided his dad's house. Mike Goodrum was angry with him (as was usually the case) for quitting his job at the warehouse, where he had health benefits, and for ducking the child support. Child support was one of the many constant issues they argued about.

The route to Bowling Green (population 50,000 and growing rapidly) is a direct trek up U.S. Highway 231, which was in the midst of a major construction project to widen it to four lanes. The highway is called Bowling Green Road in Scottsville and Scottsville Road in Bowling Green. As Luke and Brittany drove, the view of green meadows and scattered farmhouses gradually gave way to a gray sea of asphalt, car dealerships, motels, and hamburger restaurants. The towering neon fast-food signs reached up like antennas to the sky.

Farther into town, in the downtown district, was Western Kentucky University, or simply Western as most locals called it. Luke was unfamiliar with the campus, though. He only knew how to get to one of the town's only nightclubs, Good Tymes Too, which was in a refurbished pizza parlor nearby, and to the mall. When Luke would go out after Brittany had gone home for her curfew, he would venture over to Nashville, Tennessee, a half hour away, instead of to Bowling Green. There were clubs, raves, and nicer strip bars down there. It was also where most of his drug connections lived.

Luke and Brittany followed Scottsville Road to the mall and circled the parking lot before finding a space. The Greenwood Mall was orbited by megastores. The biggest, a Walmart Supercenter, encompassed, among other things, a supermarket, a McDonald's, and an optometrist's office. The area drew in shoppers from the surrounding smaller towns and was usually gridlocked.

Luke and Brittany combed the large halls of the shopping complex and stopped inside Lids, a baseball cap store. Luke bought a white Yankees cap with a blue "NY" on the front. Then they lazily browsed some more, walking hand in hand, killing time until it was late enough to dine at one of the many nearby steak houses.

They made their final lap, unaware of an eighteen-year-old Western freshman named Katie Autry, who was circling those same halls with her roommate. Katie was a complete stranger, but within a week, her name would be linked to Luke's forever.

CHAPTER 2

Katie Autry strode into the children's section of the department store. Her roommate and best friend, Danica Jackson, reluctantly trailed her. Danica found it odd but amusing that Katie had such a penchant for anything having to do with babies. Katie loved babysitting and would often stop women pushing carriages to ask how old their children were, and to coo excitedly with warmth and longing. Katie had a natural maternal inclination, and it had been evident ever since she was a little girl. Being a mother was one of Katie's biggest dreams.

Katie was blonde and Caucasian and Danica was of mixed race, half black and a quarter white and Dominican. Katie and Danica were both pretty, with shoulder-length hair and soft facial features. Katie's naturally fair skin was deeply tanned. She sunburned easily but insisted on going to the tanning bed often and wearing the strongest tanning oil. Katie had a round, cherubic face; she was more girlish than womanly. Katie had been a cheerleader in high school and she still displayed exuberance and bubbly pep, but once anyone had gotten to know her, it was evident that Katie's joy was armor. An underlying sadness pierced through—particularly when she was drinking. Katie and Danica were always together and had a reputation for being "party girls."

Katie browsed through the racks of infants' clothing.

"We're going to live down the street from each other," Katie said as she picked up a blue jumper, "and our kids are going to grow up next to each other. I'm going to have little mixed kids."

"Yeah, I'm going to be the mixed aunt!" Danica replied, laughing.

Katie and Danica would often make up humorous fantasies of their future together—like having matching bachelorette parties at Chuck E. Cheese. The girls talked about growing old together as neighbors, and Katie smiled thinking about it. Her disarming jack-o'-lantern grin (which was always coupled with her bright blue eyes squinted almost shut) was her standout feature, along with her voice. Katie's high, squeaky pitch was cartoon-like and unmistakable. She spoke with a country accent, molasses-thick, even by Kentucky standards—she said "warsh" instead of "wash."

Katie and her family hailed from Rosine, a tiny village in Ohio County 30 miles northwest of Bowling Green with a population of 41 and no stoplight. The Autrys' situation was closer to poor than comfortable, but they got by. Rosine is best known as the birthplace of the musician and songwriter Bill Monroe, the celebrated progenitor of bluegrass music. His most famous song, "Blue Moon of Kentucky," was recorded both by Elvis Presley and by Patsy Cline. Most of Monroe's songs are set among the hills of Rosine and his grave has become a tourist attraction for bluegrass aficionados who venture to this scenic, isolated town to leave mandolin and guitar picks on his headstone. Katie left Rosine when she was ten years old—the state took her and her sister away and put them into foster care.

After some mild coaxing, Danica led Katie out of the kids' section, and they went to the bedding department. Danica purchased a fluffy down comforter and carried it in its zippered, clear plastic bag. The girls went out to Danica's car, a decade-old Ford Escort. Katie didn't have a car and always depended on Danica or other friends for a ride. She couldn't stand having to ask for rides every time she wanted to go anywhere. Katie and Danica loaded the trunk with their shopping bags and drove the short distance to the neighboring cinema.

They saw *What a Girl Wants,* a movie about a girl growing up without a father. She discovers that he is in fact alive and goes to England to find him. Despite the triteness of the film, it was impossible for it not to stir up parallels to Katie's own life. Katie didn't know who her father was, and she wouldn't be finding him in England or anywhere else for that matter.

Katie's mother, Donnie, was one of seven children born to Wavie and Peggy Sue Autry. In 1984, when she was nineteen years old, Donnie gave birth to Melissa Kaye, nicknamed "Katie." Donnie named her after Melissa Gilbert, whom she liked on the TV program *Little House on the Prairie.* She didn't know who the father was. Katie's sister, Lisa, followed in 1986. In actuality, Lisa was Katie's half sister.

"Me and Katie got different dads," Lisa would remember. "We're not really so sure who Katie's dad is."

When Lisa was born, her father left. "He's in prison," Lisa says. "When I was younger I was wanting to meet my dad but now I can't really give two shits. Katie was convinced that he was her dad, too. She wanted to meet him. I know it affects me because the only father figure I had growing up was my uncles. For me, I can't get close to a man because he can't know me if my own dad don't."

The girls never referred to each other as half sisters, nor did anyone else. The bond between Katie and Lisa was stronger than sisterly; they were each other's world. Katie was a mother figure and protector to Lisa from a very early age.

CHAPTER 3

Katie began her freshman year at Western during an exciting period for Bowling Green. The strategic positioning between Nashville and Louisville, and Western's constant supply of an educated workforce, combined to make the town a prime locale for commerce. Bowling Green would later be ranked fourteenth in *Forbes*'s "Best Small Places for Business" list and was one of the small towns chosen for *National Geographic*'s "50 Best Places to Live and Play." The cost of living was cheap, and the job market vast. The unemployment rate was only 2 percent. Even the small, poorer towns surrounding Bowling Green (including Scottsville) became boons for Bowling Green's economy. If a factory chose to go to one of the satellite towns with a high unemployment rate, the wages would be spent in Bowling Green, where there were stores. It was a win-win situation.

Exit 26 off I-65 was added in the middle of town at the end of 2002 and became Bowling Green's third on-ramp to the interstate. Now the burgeoning stream of drivers pulling into town could be greeted by trees instead of McDonald's and Hardee's. Suddenly, Bowling Green became the kind of city where you would get on the interstate to go from one section to another. Construction was everywhere as new buildings and shopping centers bloomed. Counteracting the seemingly endless proliferation of twenty-four-hour pharmacies were skate parks, soccer fields, bike trails, and long stretches of green. The rusty condemned bridge over the Barren River was turned into a walkway illuminated by Chinese lanterns with a gorgeous view over the water. Some $270 million would be spent in the county annually by tourists coming to see such attractions as Lost River Cave, a national park that was a rumored hideout of Jesse James and had once been a nightclub in the 1940s.

The downtown district, where many grand old structures had been destroyed in the 1960s and '70s, was being revitalized. After years of virtual disuse, the square was again a major focal point of life, hosting festivals, weddings, concerts, and people just out for a pleasant stroll. The square is a park surrounding a black fountain ornamented with sculpted swans and children spouting water from conch shells. A brick walkway loops around it. Faux-marble statues of Roman goddesses and muses are posted around the fountain like sentries. A coffee shop was added around the perimeter of the square and apartments were renovated and rented above the shops. The square was also home to Brewing Company (nicknamed Brewco) and Darkstar, two raucous, frattish sports bars that were the main student hangouts, and the Capitol Arts Theatre, a restored art deco landmark.

But the changes to Bowling Green went beyond the never-ending construction. There was a striking shift in the makeup of the people themselves. For generations, Bowling Green was a town of black and white. The occasional minorities moved in, but they hardly registered a blip in the census. This changed in the 1990s when Bowling Green became a major hub for immigrants. Work was plentiful, Western's international draw was increasing, and the fledgling Refugee Center (now called the International Center) eagerly sought new settlers. The town now had a Little Mexico, complete with churches, markets, and ramshackle bodegas and nightclubs. A wide array of languages could be heard in the aisles of supermarkets and pharmacies; just a few years before, the sound of a foreign tongue would have turned heads and elicited stares. A huge wave of Bosnian Muslim refugees settled here and a mosque was built. A makeshift synagogue would soon take over an old law office, and a trailer in a field would be converted to a Buddhist temple. Large families of immigrants could now be seen walking across busy highways, a caravan in native dress carrying Walmart shopping bags as speeding pickups zoomed past.

The newcomers provided a much-needed jump start to culture, particularly cuisine, which was in a dire condition. Bowling Green had been overrun by large commercial chain restaurants and fast-food franchises, especially evident on Scottsville Road and 31W bypass, the two main roads that bisect the town. Local independent restaurants had all but become extinct save for a couple of "meat and three" diners, and most of the remaining home-cookin' restaurants served obviously canned fare. Almost single-handedly, the Bosnians reinvigorated if not created the food scene. They restored run-down historic houses and turned them into restaurants. The large influx of Japanese moving in because of the auto factories created restaurants where you could get sushi as good as what's found in a big city—they would pick up fresh fish flown into Nashville daily. Mexican eateries and taquerias flourished, and Thai, Indian, and Cambodian fare further diversified the scene.

The yearly International Festival attracted upwards of thirteen thousand people to the square to witness such spectacles as native Filipino dancing, reggae, Celtic music, and South American crafts.

The South is traditionally a place where foreign ancestry is forgotten or willfully buried, no matter how ethnic a last name sounds. There isn't the clinging to heritage as those do in the North, parading for cultures no matter how large the disconnect to the motherland. One is first and foremost an American and a Kentuckian here. "What's your background" just wasn't asked before the 1990s.

For a small southern town, Bowling Green already had an open-minded and cosmopolitan quality to it because of the university. But a large, rapid influx of immigrants in a small town setting couldn't happen without problems. The Hispanic population increased in Warren County by 42 percent from 2000 to 2006. Many saw this as an invasion. Soon 12 percent of public school students were studying English as a Second Language, with more than twenty different languages being spoken. This was a major obstacle for the school budget and teacher training. Racist graffiti was sprayed on some houses and on a bridge. A cross was burned in the yard of a Latino family, and Ku Klux Klan literature started appearing in mailboxes and was even passed out at the mall. Immigrant gangs such as the BH Boys from Bosnia and Herzegovina, and various Latin and Asian street groups formed. The Latin population didn't tend to assimilate as well as other immigrant groups. The education level in their native countries was lower than many of the other incoming refugees, and unlike the Bosnians, they couldn't physically pass as white southerners. Many worried that the poor newcomers were siphoning local resources. The census counted 6,631 immigrants in 2007, but the figure was probably three times that number, according to the director of the International Center. Of those accounted for, 4,932 weren't naturalized citizens. Tension was pervasive, especially among older generations of locals who weren't used to living in a multicultural atmosphere.

As the demographics of neighborhoods changed and new ethnic enclaves formed, gated communities proliferated. A gorgeous, guarded upper-class neighborhood called Olde Stone was built across a bridge around a country club and pro-level golf course. The socioeconomic level of Olde Stone shifted slightly, to the residents' chagrin, when a Scottsville trailer park resident won a house in a charity raffle. Classes were becoming distinct. Unlike Scottsville, where the wealthy Turners would frequent the same places as other citizens, Bowling Green was becoming increasingly stratified. The small town was on the verge of becoming a city, seemingly overnight.

CHAPTER 4

After the movie, Danica and Katie drove back to campus. Western is a sprawling school whose oldest buildings, including a Greek-style amphitheater, a rustic log cabin, and an antebellum mansion housing the Kentucky Museum, spiral around a hill like Mount Olympus—giving the student body its nickname, the Hilltoppers. Western is symbiotically connected to Bowling Green: the town's economy depends on the university, with its fifteen thousand students and its jobs. The school is the largest local employer. A water tower, painted like an American flag, looms atop a nearby hill and watches over the university. Visible for miles outside the town's borders, the water tower is famous throughout the region. It appears in the opening montage of the evening news and has graced the cover of the phone book.

At an ever-increasing rate, Western outgrew its hill and enveloped the land around it. Much of Western stands on what was once Jonesville, an African-American community that formed after the Civil War. With slavery dismantled, the area thrived. However, in 1955 the school started purchasing plots of land in the neighboring Jonesville district for expansion. Many landowners held out, but in 1964 the quarter was condemned, despite the protests of the residents. WKU bought the land at a much-reduced price and leveled the buildings.

One of the buildings constructed adjacent to the Jonesville site in 1969 was Hugh Poland Hall, an imposing, monolithic brick structure. The eight-story tower's design is clinical, uninviting, and anonymous, and the place could easily be mistaken for a nursing home or hospital. This was where Katie and Danica lived.

Poland was a coed residence hall with alternating floors for male and female, a collegiate parfait. Residents on each floor shared a set of bathrooms. A quad linking Poland to other dorms was always crowded with students. Outside, on the street level, students would holler up to the open windows to summon their friends. In summer, girls would lie out on colorful beach towels to tan. The sidewalks were always busy with students going to and from class and trudging the long distances to the vast parking lots.

Before moving in with each other, Katie and Danica both had roommates with whom they didn't get along. Katie's first roommate, who was black, would often deride her in front of her friends for sleeping around—especially when it was with black guys. Their last confrontation concerned Katie sleeping with a guy that her roommate was dating. The girl threw a hairbrush at Katie for the indiscretion, followed by a series of epithets and profanities.

Sexual experimentation is frequently promoted now among college-age women, yet it can still bring derision as well. Liberation and objectification are both subjective. Katie gained a reputation in the dorm for being promiscuous. Some of the guys nicknamed her "the ho of the second flo.'" At this stage when most experiment with their sexuality, Katie had sex not as a way of making herself happy, but as a way of pleasing others. It was a form of subservience as well as a compulsion. Katie often regretted sleeping with a guy, and it was a difficult lesson to learn that sex wouldn't make guys like her. Katie confessed to a friend that she had never had an orgasm. For her, sex seemed to give the illusion, however fleeting, of being appreciated, loved, and beautiful, and of not being alone.

Danica had seen Katie, who lived two doors down from her, in passing in the hallway or at the communal floor bathroom. Danica initially misread Katie's shyness and quietness as her being stuck-up. They ended up becoming acquainted at a dining hall the night after the hairbrush incident and exchanged woes about their living situations. The solution was quite obvious, and Katie moved in two days later. After a week, they were inseparable and finishing each other's sentences.

"What are you, the freakin' Bobbsey Twins?" one of their friends asked them.

Both Katie and Danica usually only hung out with guys, so it was great to have a girlfriend to depend on. They would stay in their dorm room together and watch reruns of *The Golden Girls* and talk and listen to music late into the night. They opened up to each other. Danica recalls Katie telling her she was a virgin until just before college. "She didn't want to come to college a virgin," Danica says. "She thought everybody would laugh at her."

Although they overlapped every now and then, Danica and Katie had different tastes in boys. "She had a thing for football players," Danica says. "She liked big muscles. I like cocky boys because I like to take them down a notch, knock them down a little bit. She liked guys to dominate her, to tell her what to do. It was like she didn't know what to do if nobody told her what to do. If a truck was coming at her and you didn't tell her to move she would just stand there and panic."

Danica grew up around Elizabethtown, Kentucky, and was quite close to her mother. Her father wasn't really in her life. Danica's mother, Donna Jackson, thought that Katie sounded like a little girl when she answered the phone. But as time went on, Donna Jackson wasn't able to tell Katie's voice apart from her own daughter's.

The winter that they met, Katie went to Elizabethtown with Danica for a weekend visit. Danica's mother came home from work and saw two tiny sneakers by the front door.

"Danica, is there a child here?" she called out, thinking that one of the neighborhood children was there for some reason.

"No, that's Katie's shoes!" Danica responded loudly from down the hall.

Donna went to Danica's bedroom and opened the door. "Katie was sitting in the middle of the bed with her legs crossed," she remembers. "She looked up and she had this smile from ear to ear, just like sunshine."

Danica's mother took the girls to dinner at O'Charley's. Katie ate slowly and delicately, picking at her food in small, ladylike bites. Donna was charmed by Katie. She found Katie sweet and gentle, a nice, quiet foil for her daughter, who covered her sensitive side with brazenness. The girls were quite different, she thought, but they had the same sense of humor, always laughing, and there was never a lull in their conversation.

With each passing day, Katie became more headstrong. This personality shift was jarring for many who had known her for a long time, and these stabs at self-sufficiency were often counterproductive if not downright detrimental. Like most college freshmen, Katie was dabbling with strikingly different personas—the diligent worker, the sexualized party girl, the sensitive waif. As Katie matured, these character facets might coalesce into her adult identity. She was finding out who she was on her own terms. Many attributed Katie's marked new autonomy to Danica. For her part, Danica was relieved that Katie was finally sticking up for herself and doing what she wanted. Katie's helplessness exasperated Danica. When they had first met, Katie let people walk all over her in a manner that Danica would never tolerate.

Katie's ongoing transition to independence culminated when she had herself rescinded from foster care. Although eighteen years old, Katie was eligible to remain in foster care, and collect the benefits thereof, until she turned twenty-one. Katie filed the documents herself to be released from care and Danica drove her to the hearing just the month before. As part of Kentucky's foster care program, Katie's tuition to Western had been waived. Katie reduced her classes to part-time enrollment and worked more hours at her job at the smoothie shop in the student center. She and Danica put down a deposit for an off-campus apartment to live in the following school year. Katie was now officially her own person.

Katie was always very quiet about her life before she moved in with her foster parents, the Inmans. Little by little, bits of information would slip out, but Danica could never put the puzzle together exactly. Katie told Danica that her birth mother, Donnie, was "sick," and she wouldn't go into it further. Katie and Donnie were still in contact, though, and Danica would hear Katie speaking to her mother from time to time on the phone. It seemed that she would always have to repeat herself during the calls and would inevitably finish them frustrated. Katie called both her foster mother, Shirley Inman, and her birth mother "Mom."

"As we grew closer, I found out more about her," Danica recalled, "like along the lines of why she was in foster care. She never really gave a specific reason. I remember her telling me before her and Lisa were born her mom was normal. It's like something just kind of snowballed. When I met her mother, I knew something was wrong. It was like she was just on a different plane, like high or something."

Danica remembered Katie telling her that one day when she was young she couldn't wake her mother up in the afternoon when she and Lisa were hungry. Katie nearly cut her finger off trying to slice a fruit roll-up in two to feed herself and Lisa.

When she was in her twenties, Donnie Autry's behavior drastically changed.

"She wasn't the Donnie we were used to her being," her sister, Virginia White, explains. "We knew there was a difference. When a person starts behaving and acting differently then that's where doctors come in."

Donnie was exhibiting the symptoms of schizophrenia. It is something that the family does not like to discuss (Virginia can be agitatedly defensive on the matter). They vaguely refer to her condition in passing as "Donnie's illness" and don't offer specifics about what exactly happened in the household.

"When my momma was little she had some symptoms of schizophrenia," Lisa says, "like talking to nobody. I think when she had her tubes cut and tied that's what really brought it out. That's what my mom said. She had a partial hysterectomy."

Donnie's condition triggered the first of many relocations for the sisters. Donnie first took the girls to live with her at her parents' house. She was soon overwhelmed by her sickness, and required one of what would turn out to be many hospitalizations. The girls were placed with their aunt Virginia, who raised them for a time along with her daughter, Barbie, breaking all three from the bottle at the same time.

"Donnie got better," Virginia says, "and of course she wanted her girls back. They're her kids so I did. And there was I guess a complication in the medicines or whatever because I don't understand how the illness works so I'm not qualified to say anything about the illness. I am not a doctor. Barbie is not a doctor. All I know is I know Donnie. I know my sister and I love her. She became ill again and another family relative tried to keep them. At that time I had something else going on in my life."

In May 1993, Donnie and Virginia's other sister, Barbara, filed a petition to be the girls' guardian. The application states:

"Mother has recently been released from Western State Hospital and is unable to provide care for this child. Mother has had numerous hospitalizations and upon return has demonstrated she cannot maintain stability and provide appropriate care."

"We stayed with my aunt Barbara and her husband," Lisa recalls hazily. "But then my uncle went to the social worker and that's how we got into foster care. I don't know. They got divorced. Mom had to go to the hospital for her illness."

Katie and Lisa were placed with foster parents in Pellville, Kentucky.

CHAPTER 5

There is a raw, unbridled quality to the landscape of Pellville. It looks untamable; vast craggy woods give way to endless fields. The man-made and the natural clash with a begrudged equilibrium. Rough rocky hills are sprinkled with trailer homes, many collapsed, burnt down into husks, and left to weather away slowly. Long stretches of woods are interrupted by the rusting bodies of cast-off cars. Ancient trucks, farming equipment, and other debris decorate the sides of the road. Unused trampolines with rusted springs block the sunlight and create circles of dirt. A seemingly disproportionate number of modest churches, all Baptist, dot the scenery.

This western coal fields town is where Katie lived for ten years or so before coming to Bowling Green for college. Hancock County, population 8,000 and 98 percent white, comprises a triumvirate of towns: Lewisport, Hawesville, and the smallest, Pellville. When Katie and Lisa arrived, Pellville had little more than a gas station and a post office. The post office has since closed.

The girls were placed with Jim and Shirley Inman, a couple in their sixties whose own children were grown.

The Inmans had taken in many foster kids before. Jim Inman, a retired air force lieutenant colonel, had flown in missions over Laos and Vietnam. After twenty-two years of service, he settled his family in Hancock County and became the director of the county's Emergency Management Services. The Inmans are well-known and respected within the community and are particularly religious, attending groups and services at their Baptist church throughout the week.

For the first time, religion was a part of Katie's and Lisa's everyday lives. The girls had brand-new, much older foster parents (and their first father figure, who was ex-military) and a new town, and they had lost everything and everybody they had known. Their socioeconomic standing also shifted. They were now living in a two-story house and were thoroughly provided for. All of this was a lot to handle for two young girls who had become accustomed to fluidity in their lives.

"For a while they didn't click too well," says a friend of the family. "They would always be getting in trouble for something."

Katie and Lisa eventually adapted to the nuclear-family life, and came to call Jim and Shirley "Dad" and "Mom." Katie and Lisa referred to the Inmans' extended family as cousins, aunts, and uncles, as though they were blood relatives.

As a child, Katie played in the pond on the property and caught turtles with her "cousin" Justin Briggs, the stepson of one of the Inmans' sons. Justin and Katie played pranks on Lisa. Once they dared Lisa to go into a camper, saying that there was a ghost inside, and then locked her in.

Already closer than most siblings, the upheaval bound Katie and Lisa even tighter. No matter how much everything changed around them, they always had each other.

Lisa's loving nickname for Katie was "Sissy." Katie pretended to hate it, but Lisa called her that anyway. Although there was now a solid mother figure in their lives, the role of surrogate never diminished for Katie. This unbreakable bond between the two could also make it harder for a new foster mom to connect with them.

"Katie watched over Lisa," says Ashley Napier, a friend of the sisters. "She wouldn't let anybody pick on her. They was best friends, too. They would do anything for each other."

The girls got to see more of the country and travel outside of Kentucky to visit the Inmans' family. They went to places like North Dakota and Oklahoma, where they saw the world's largest McDonald's. Unfortunately, the radio would be tuned in to country stations for these fifteen-hour jaunts, while their own musical tastes ran toward Guns N' Roses and AC/DC.

As Katie and Lisa entered Hancock County High School (enrollment four hundred), tensions with their foster parents mounted. This happens to most teenagers, but it was more acute due to the wide generation gap between the girls and the Inmans. Katie dealt with this disconnect through obedience instead of rebellion. She had good grades and was on the honor roll. She wasn't the smartest person in class, but she was a hard worker and always studied. Her school activities were extensive, perhaps her way of trying to fit in. Besides cheerleading, she participated in track, the pep, Spanish, and reading clubs, and other groups such as Students Against Drunk Driving and Future Christian Athletes. Among her other achievements were Academic All-State, Honor Roll, Student of the Month, and Perfect Attendance. The list goes on and on.

No matter how hard Katie and Lisa strove to fit in, they always felt that to their peers they were just "foster children," that their poorer background before life with the Inmans equated them with being low class. Nor did they feel that they really belonged at the Inmans' house. What had defined them growing up was that they belonged nowhere and were always moving to a new place; permanence was alien. They didn't voice these feelings to anyone but each other. They also thought that they stood out to their classmates because the rules that they had to abide by were seemingly from another era. Within the home there were rigid strictures that made it feel like a transitory place for them, that they were just guests. For instance, they had to ask permission to eat and to watch television.

"Me and Katie stayed upstairs all the time," Lisa says, "and they got mad at us, because they'd say, 'You don't talk to us all that much.' Well what is there to talk about?"

Since their arrival, Katie and Lisa had made their own cocoon world in the bedroom.

"When we was younger we used to play Barbie," Lisa says. "We built dollhouses out of cardboard boxes. But when we got older, we sat in the room and talked about all kinds of stuff, made fun of each other, and talked about boys and life in general and all our problems. Katie liked watching these homemakin' shows and craft shows on TV. She'd get all this stuff out and try to make it. And as soon as she's done, she just leaves it right there. And she makes little sister pick it up! So you can always tell when Katie's seen a craft show, because there would be all this stuff everywhere."

There were firm rules about socializing and dating (both were outlawed). Their activities could consist of school and church functions and nothing else.

"Our teenage years wasn't like most teenagers," Lisa says. "Me and Katie was living like five-year-olds."

Katie began to manifest the dueling public and private personae that would become more prominent in college.

"Katie was different at school than she was at home," Justin Briggs says. "She would flirt with the guys and this and that, but in front of Jim and Shirley she would act like she wasn't interested."

"She was reserved and conservative," Briggs continues. "She wasn't into the party scene or things like that. I'd say half the reason was because of rules at home and the other half was she was focused on succeeding. She kind of just stuck her head in the books."

Katie became an accomplished cheerleader and Lisa ran track. They loved their respective sports and excelled, and the practices allowed them to get out of the house. Petite Katie was a "flyer," and would be held aloft during routines and tossed into the air, a soaring streak of red and white.

Jared Woods was Katie's stunt partner on the Hancock County Hornets' cheer squad. He would throw tiny Katie into the air and catch her on his hands.

"She was kinda shy at first," Woods remembers. "In a crowd of people she would always hang back. She wasn't confident by herself. But in cheerleading she always had to show confidence because she had to be a leader. There was almost a double personality between cheerleader Katie and just regular Katie.

"She was real funny," Woods says, "but she didn't let you know that at first. She was almost a smart-ass. She would just smile and say the most off-the-wall things and blatant things that most people wouldn't find funny. She liked to make fun of people, but in a good way. I don't think she had a mean bone in her body."

"She was always the perfect kind of girl," says Jeremiah Reeves, Justin Briggs's cousin (and therefore Katie's "cousin," too). "She had good grades. She didn't seem as edgy as the other high school girls who were all partying and having fun. She always seemed really calm and collected. She seemed to stick to herself more; she was really quiet, really soft-spoken. I've never heard her yell. She really was sweet and innocent in a way."

Briggs remembers her as socially adept and not adhering to cliques. "She hung out with the popular girls and everything," he recalls, "but she wasn't the type to just be with that group. She would hang out with everybody. When you're kids it's like 'I'm a cheerleader, I can't hang out with the nerds or that fat girl over there.' She wasn't like that."

A recent transplant to Hancock County, Heather McMahon, roomed with Katie at cheerleading camp the summer of their freshman year. Heather became a "base" on the squad; at five feet eight she was one of the taller girls and helped to support the others when doing a pyramid and to hurl flyers like Katie when performing stunts.

The first night at camp, they stayed up talking past midnight. "When she would talk," Heather says, "it was like everything she said was so important. She always had that tone in her voice, like it was this really special thing that she was talking about."

Katie and Heather felt like newcomers and outsiders in Pellville and were glad to find each other.

"Most people that lived there grew up there," Heather says. "They were born there. Everyone became friends in elementary school and stayed friends all the way up. She wasn't born and raised there, so that did help link us because we did have that connection. We both understood what it was like."

"I was told," Heather's father, Sean McMahon, recalls, " 'No matter how long you live here, you will never be considered a local. If your kids stay here and marry some-one local, their kids will be locals.' It's kind of clannish."

Heather would go to Katie's house as often as she could. "Her mom didn't like us hanging out a lot. Her mom thought she needed to be home studying and stuff, so she and I didn't get to go out a lot on the weekends."

When the girls could see each other over the weekend, they would usually stay in and stay up late listening to music and talking. Heather and Katie would often go to the school dances together. There wasn't really any point in getting a date when they'd be cheering throughout the homecoming game anyway. Sometimes they'd get photos made together in front of the seasonal backdrops.

Just before senior year, Heather found out that her fa-ther was taking a job in Florida. She and Katie cried for two days straight. They had been inseparable for two years, and Katie had never been as close to anyone except for Lisa.

"We were friendly with everyone," Heather says of her and Katie's social life, "but neither one of us had another person that we were super close to. She kinda knew when I left that she was going to have friends and she was going to have people to be there for her but she wasn't going to have someone that she was going to talk to seven times a day. We talked to each other about everything. She wasn't the type of person who was a loner; she was the type of person who had friends and who wanted friends and wanted to be the friendly person."

When Heather left, Katie had to begin a new chapter in her life. "She was still the same person but she kept to herself more after Heather moved," Briggs remembers.

Katie added to her after-school activities a job at Wen-dy's, a fast-food restaurant right across the Ohio River from Hawesville in Tell City, Indiana. Coming back into

Kentucky from Tell City, one is greeted by a neon cross atop a tall, tree-covered hill in the distance. The cross looks like shining platinum piercing the gray clouds on a misty day and Katie must have gazed at it on the ride home from work.

Heather and Katie had always talked about going to college together. "Katie wanted to be a dental hygienist," Heather says. "That was always her thing. Who thinks of that in high school? When she would get an idea in her head she would think it was the most important thing and she wanted everyone to think it's the most important. She had her heart set on it."

Heather's life in Florida became quite different than the one she had shared with Katie. Eventually, Heather moved in with a boyfriend and didn't want to return to Kentucky. Katie found out that Western Kentucky University in Bowling Green had a good dental program.

Before her first semester of college began, Katie went to Destin, Florida, as part of an all-female church youth outing. She hadn't seen Heather, who lived about twenty minutes from Destin, in two years, but they would still not have a reunion.

"Her mother made her promise that she wouldn't come see me," Heather says. "She even told the counselor not to let Katie see me. The only thing I can think of is her mom just didn't want her to get into any trouble, and evidently me living with a guy who I wasn't married to was trouble. Apparently her mother didn't want her to be around people that could influence her like that."

CHAPTER 6

When they returned from the movie, Katie and Danica entered fortresslike Poland Hall and went to their room, number 214. Their door was decorated with various seasonal construction paper name tags that had outlasted their corresponding holidays. "Katie" was written in black marker on a heart, an Easter egg, and on a green leaf. A pumpkin and a snowman were labeled "Danica." A "Katie" turkey roosted a few inches away from a "Danica" Christmas tree.

Their dorm room was what one would expect—two twin beds, two dressers, and two desks, all crammed within inhospitable cinder-block walls covered in photographs and magazine cutouts. The eleven-by-seven-foot room always had heaps of clothes on the floor—Danica wasn't much for straightening up, and ever acquiescent, Katie just let Danica's mess take over.

The girls took a nap, their beds separated by just a few feet. The rest was good for Danica. Something had been bothering her all day, and she wasn't exactly sure what it was. She just knew that something wasn't right. It was a subtle twinge, though, a pang so slight she couldn't fully grasp it.

Katie awoke hungry. The ceiling above her bed was covered in stickers of stars. A smoke alarm and a metal pipe running along the ceiling ending in a sprinkler interrupted the adhesive galaxy.

Katie took Danica's keys to borrow her car to grab some dinner. Once safely out of Danica's earshot, Katie called Maurice Perkins on her cell phone.

"I'm getting ready to go get some food. Do you want anything?" she asked him.

"Where are you going?"

"Arby's."

"Can you get me a sandwich and some curly fries?"

Maurice wasn't Katie's boyfriend, but he was more than a friend. However, "seeing each other" was too strong a term. They were "talking" or "hanging out." There was a multitude of vague slang terms that could be used to describe their intimate relationship. Maurice, in fact, had a girlfriend who lived out of town. The girl actually found out about Katie and sent her a threatening email saying that she wished she would go to sleep and never wake up. Maurice and Katie's liaison might have been casual, but as often happens in such circumstances, the feelings of one outgrew the other's. Katie thought that she loved him.

"Maurice was her main infatuation," one of Katie's friends recalls. "He was a typical guy that had a beautiful girl and didn't want a serious relationship. The relationship in her mind was not the same relationship that he had in his mind."

Maurice had been a high school sports star in his hometown of Indianapolis and was majoring in computer science at Western, where he was also a standout wide-receiver. Maurice was five-nine and weighed 170 pounds, somewhat slight for a collegiate football player. He walked with his feet spread shoulder-width apart and had the powerful gait of an athlete. He had a broad and boyish face and often kept his mouth closed when he smiled, possibly to hide the gap between his two front teeth. He spoke with the smooth confidence of someone used to doing well with the opposite sex and wore a diamond stud in each earlobe.

Because she came from a town with an infinitesimal black population (there was a single black student in her high school), it surprised some of Katie's friends that she was open-minded about mixed-race relationships.

"Part of it was growing up the way she did," Danica says, "seeing a lot of things early on—episodes with her mom and being placed from home to home put her in a place where she wasn't as judgmental as other people."

Over time, the stigma of mixed-race relationships has lessened in Kentucky, but for many they are certainly still taboo. Danica thought Katie was discovering her natural predilections, but that it was also a way of rebelling.

"I was the third or fourth black she had 'talked' to," Maurice says. "I think she was a little hesitant of that. Most white girls who've never dated a black guy hesitate going into that. It's a lot different down here. It's not like students walked around and looked at us wrong or anything. But if you were at the mall or something and an older couple saw you, they would look at you like 'What's going on?' I asked her, 'Would your parents be cool with you dating a black guy?' And she was like, 'Probably not.' I was like, 'Well, I understand. Kentucky, small town, probably no black people there.'"

Maurice and Katie had met the previous October at the smoothie shop where Katie worked. She went to Maurice's dorm room later that night when he had a few friends over. Katie was quiet and reserved, but in good spirits.

"She was real giggly," Maurice remembers. "Whenever she laughed I would just die laughing because her laugh was just so . . . country! That's what really attracted me to her was her laugh. She laughed all the time."

Katie became a frequent presence at Perkins's dorm, hanging out and playing video games—she was absolutely terrible at them. She became part of the group, or as Maurice says, "one of da fellahs."

When Katie arrived at Maurice's dorm to drop off the food the sun was setting and the sky was pink and crimson. Maurice came downstairs and Katie handed him the sack. She asked for a kiss on the cheek and he obliged. Katie couldn't stay long because she was breaking one of Danica's main rules about her car: it was not to be used to visit Maurice.

Danica did not like Maurice and the feeling was mutual. Maurice thought that Danica partied too much and was a bad influence. Danica thought that Maurice used Katie and selfishly accepted the gifts Katie showered on him despite her not being able to afford them—video games, clothes, shoes, just about anything he wanted. Katie always seemed to be crying about him, and her weakness for Maurice exasperated Danica.

"He never wants to take me out on a date!" Katie would whine.

"Fine! Move on! Let's just date ourselves!" Danica would respond sharply.

Katie would always hassle Maurice for one of his shirts. She wanted just one item, a souvenir of him, something to represent him and always have with her and make him real and solid and physical when he wasn't there. Maurice didn't understand this, although Katie was not the first girl who insisted on taking his clothes. He would say no and Katie would cry and think he was being mean and this would invariably set off Danica. Maurice finally gave Katie a large turquoise T-shirt and she lovingly wore it each night to sleep.

Maurice did do nice things for Katie, though. Katie was always in need of a ride, so Maurice often chauffered her. He would often pick Katie up from her new job. However, he had been shocked when he found out what she wanted to do.

The club Tattle Tails is on the edge of town, between the interstate and the river, and attracts a hodgepodge clientele of college students, local toughs, Japanese businessmen, and just about everything in between. On weekend nights the gravel parking lot is filled with pickup trucks and SUVs. It is a ramshackle, grayish-blue, one-story building with a mud-brown roof. Hot pink decorative columns accentuate the façade and match the two separate front doors. The building is divided down the middle into two sections: one is for drinking, the other for watching ladies. After a patron finishes his drink he must walk outside and go through the adjacent door to the pole dancing area. This is because of a city ordinance that prohibits doing the two activities simultaneously. Those under twenty-one can frequent the stripping section but can't go into the other room. Another local law bans the exposure of a woman's nipples—dancers at Tattle Tails abide by this regulation with just the right amount of strategically placed duct tape.

In April, Katie and Danica came in looking for work and started soon after. Katie's original goal of working at Tattle Tails was to earn enough money for a car. She wanted to buy the cheapest Dodge Neon she could find, and she could earn a lot more in a short time stripping than she would at the smoothie shop. But there must have been more psychological than monetary reasoning, conscious or unconscious, to make someone like Katie embark upon stripping. The transition of Katie from shy and sheltered to an exhibitionist was striking. This would have been the ultimate rebellion for Katie. But by dancing, this was also a safe, illusionary way of straying from her pious adolescence—she was neither fully nude nor engaging in prostitution or anything else more extreme. She could exude and explore confidence, a quality that by most accounts she didn't have in everyday life. It also gave her the feeling of control, empowerment, and the sensation of being loved, even if these boons were ever so fleeting and ultimately illusions. But for a college-age woman, it was also something of a lark, slumming in an era where just about anything can be mistaken as female empowerment.

Katie's first outing onstage was awkward. She had some drinks beforehand, and paired a sheer white wrap with a thong. She had no moves planned, and just kind of wiggled nervously. Getting onstage got easier. Katie would unwrap the sarong from her waist and outstretch it like wings, her tiny feet in high heels, her body gorgeous and small, yet curvy. Common to the profession, the dancers at Tattle Tails used stage names like Summer, Alexia, and Shimmer. Katie became "Crystal."

Katie was popular with the clientele. They tipped her on the runway by slipping dollar bills into the elastic of her g-string and paid extra for private dances. Unlike some of the dancers who generally attracted a certain type, Katie's admirers encompassed all races and ages. Oftentimes, Katie wouldn't even have to dance, the men just wanted to talk to her.

One regular patron, a high school senior, asked Katie to his prom. Not knowing how to politely decline, Katie said yes, but later backed out of going.

"Why would he want to take a stripper to his prom?" Katie asked Danica.

Katie made a few hundred dollars a night, more than the other dancers. This amount went a long way in Bowling Green, where a nice apartment could be rented for around three hundred dollars a month.

In this setting, the roles of extrovert and introvert were reversed for Danica and Katie. Danica worked twice at the club and that was enough for her; she mostly spent her tenure goofing off with Katie. Danica didn't want Katie telling anyone about them working there, and Katie agreed to keep it secret. But Katie wasn't ashamed of her job and let it slip to a few people, even some of her best friends back home in Pellville. She also told her birth mother, Donnie, and Aunt Virginia, who were slightly concerned, but took her employment in stride. "God gave you your body and when you came into the world you were naked," reasoned Virginia. They were more apprehensive of her crossing the parking lot late at night alone.

In a way Katie was proud that she could be sexy and receive this kind of admiration. Most people she had told that she was stripping thought she was joking. No one could believe that cheerleader Katie could become a stripper. She had to tell her boss at the smoothie shop three times before he would believe her.

CHAPTER 7

After eating at the steak house, Brittany and Luke wanted to get some alcohol to take home to Scottsville, which is in a dry county. They pulled into Vette City Liquors, a nondescript, weathered box of a building with a neon sign of a red Corvette in front.

Bowling Green is known as the "Corvette Capital of the World," home to the sport car's only factory. The National Corvette Museum is a big tourist draw, the police fleet boasts a Corvette squad car, and Big Red, Western's furry blob of a mascot, peels out in basketball games during halftime in his own mini 'Vette. The annual Corvette Parade draws connoisseurs from around the country, and CNN often broadcasts the honking procession.

Luke went inside the liquor store and picked up a twelve-pack of Rolling Rock for himself and some bottles of fruit-flavored tequila coolers for Brittany, who didn't like the taste of beer.

As Luke and Brittany pulled into Scottsville, a stark billboard on a hill greeted them. In white lettering painted on a black background is written a selection of the Ten Commandments:

Thou Shalt Not Commit Adultery
Thou Shalt Not Kill
Thou Shalt Not Steal
Thou Shalt Not Bear False Witness
Thou Shalt Not Covet

There are other such signs positioned throughout the town, usually standing inexplicably in fields, their messages more haunting and abstract as you drive deeper into Allen County. On top of a lonely shorn embankment a massive placard reads:

Jesus Said You Be Ashamed of Me
and I Will Be Ashamed of You

Cows grazing in a pasture are reminded:

HERE awaits heartfelt salvation

Despite being only about half an hour away from the much larger Bowling Green, there is a sense of isolation and independence in Scottsville. It's not considered a suburb. If you don't live in Scottsville, there isn't much of a reason to go there. There is no mall, no movie theater even. Many from Bowling Green have never been there at all even though it's just down the road. But Scottsville is not without its charms. There are a couple of "home-cookin'" restaurants serving food like fried chicken, greens, and corncakes, fare that has all but disappeared in Bowling Green. Quaint houses line the streets, and there is a sense of permanence that Bowling Green, the ever-evolving neighbor whose concrete borders creep closer each year, lacks.

Centered around a downtown square, Scottsville retains an old-fashioned small town charm. If it weren't for the modern automobiles lining the streets and the fluorescent pink and orange hazard signs on the backs of the sizable Amish community's horse-drawn carriages, it could very well be a film set for another decade. The surrounding landscape can be breathtaking. Lush, hilly, green fields, farmland, valleys that trap the mist, and woods surround the town from all sides. Long country highways snake out from the square, the view occasionally interrupted by a silo, bait shop, or one of the religious billboards. Not surprisingly in a small town like this, the locals are bound by both a sense of community and family. Many clans have been here for generations, as the familiar surnames in the graveyards can attest.

The weekly newspaper reports residents' vacations and goings-on, high school sports, and pageantry. But in recent years, the crime blotter column has required more space. The typical charges have evolved beyond petty car break-ins and public intoxication to include the production and possession of methamphetamine—a plague, along with the painkiller oxycodone, sweeping rural America.

The remoteness of the countryside in Allen County has proved a boon for meth labs; hard-to-get-to barns and abandoned farmhouses are easy to adapt to illicit use. The growing drug problem is a symptom of modernity, and for many, drugs can be a form of escapism amid bleak economic prospects.

The roughly four thousand residents are predominantly blue-collar workers. During lunch hour, restaurant patrons are mostly attired in work clothes like coveralls. Scottsville is home to a few factories, including the jelly maker Smucker's, yet almost a quarter of the population lives below the poverty line. Most of the jobs available are in the plants, but those positions are dwindling steadily due to outsourcing.

When Luke and Brittany arrived back at the apartment, Luke's roommate of three months, Matt Hire, a skinny eighteen-year-old with a scraggly goatee, was watching television with his girlfriend and another couple. Luke and Matt had met when they both worked at the Dollar General warehouse. They were civil rather than close; they rarely socialized outside of the apartment. Luke grudgingly respected Matt, though.

Luke remembers Matt with awe. "I lived with him a couple of months and he probably brought in ten girls he fucked—that I know he fucked 'cause I was there. Really, he was kind of nerdy, but for some reason the chicks dig him. I thought he was very pimpish."

Shortly after their arrival, Luke and Brittany retired to the bedroom. They had sex and then dozed off with the lights on.

Covered with sweat, Luke awoke shortly with thirst. His arm was around Brittany as they lay on the double mattress on the floor; it nearly took up the entire room. A TV rested on a wooden end table and a plastic set of drawers sat next to it. Stacked on top were a bottle of Nyquil, deodorant, lightbulbs, motor oil, and sundry other items.

Matt and the others were still in the similarly Spartan den watching television. The walls were bare, and there was little else in the room besides a recliner. Seated in it were stuffed Scooby-Doo characters, a flourish of Matt's that Luke hated.

Luke gulped down a glass of water in the kitchen. He then realized he hadn't gotten any calls that night, nor heard his cell phone ring, which was a rarity. He returned to his room to search for his phone. Brittany was waking up. She gave him her cell phone to call his own, but they couldn't hear it. It had to be in Brittany's car, Luke thought. He put on his Timberland boots and walked outside to her Maxima. Luke peered under the passenger seat and found it.

Luke was walking into the house when he noticed that the screen on Brittany's phone read: "1 missed call." Below it was printed the number of the caller, and Luke recognized it as Scott's. Scott was Luke's age and lived in a trailer in the woods where Luke would sometimes go to drink. Luke got angry. He knew that other guys were always trying to sleep with Brittany, but this was someone whom he had thought of as a friend, or at least a "buddy." Luke's jaw tightened and he called the number back using Brittany's phone.

"Why the hell you callin' the phone and shit?" Luke demanded loudly. "What are you tryin' to start?"

Scott denied calling Brittany, but Luke was relentless. The conversation didn't become more amicable. Scott told Luke that his friend had called Brittany from his phone solely to ask her about her sister, with whom he had had a relationship. This didn't quell Luke's building rage.

"I'm gonna kick your ass!" Scott yelled finally, having enough of Luke's never-ending rant.

"Well, come on then!" Luke responded. "You know where I live, out by the ballpark! Come on!"

Luke stormed into the house past the two couples perched in the living room. He swung open the bedroom door and it crashed loudly as it hit the wall. His face was red.

"Why the hell has Scott been callin' you?"

"He ain't!" Brittany replied loudly.

"There ain't no reason to lie! If that's the way it is you can leave!"

Luke called her a whore. Brittany hurriedly gathered her belongings. Luke ordered her to stay, but she didn't pause. The yelling back and forth increased and got louder.

When it reached its crescendo, Luke whipped his arm back and threw the mobile phone at Brittany, hitting her on the arm. Then he smacked her in the face.

"Fuck you!" Brittany screamed as she lunged at him.

She yanked the bandanna folded around Luke's forehead down to his neck and pulled, slapping his face with the other hand.

Brittany later told the police that Luke "slapped her and pushed her on the bed. He then straddled her and struck her twice more in the face."

She ran outside and Luke followed, trailed by the others.

"Fuck you motherfucker you stupid son of a bitch I'll call the cops on you!" Brittany cried.

Brittany got into her car and buckled the seat belt. Luke swung open the driver's side door, and to everyone's surprise, especially Brittany's, quickly spun around, aimed his backside, and sat on her. There was plenty of room since she drove with her seat pushed so far back.

Brittany struggled but was pinned down. The seat belt dug into her neck and burned. Her right arm, not pinned down by Luke's bulk, flailed helplessly like a penguin wing. Neighbors peered out of the windows.

Brittany would later say that during the ensuing struggle Luke choked her and she couldn't breathe or scream. She said that she struck Luke as hard as she could in the face but her punches had no effect, and he continued choking her until Matt's girlfriend yelled at him.

Luke raised himself from her lap, and Brittany slammed the door, put the car into reverse, and was soon gone.

Luke was shaking, both nervous and angry. Police sirens wailed in the distance. Unsure if he was the cause or if they were heading for something else, Luke didn't want to chance it. He went inside, grabbed his car keys, and sped off to his father's house in the thundering Mustang. Luckily, Luke's father and stepmother weren't home when he got there.

Inside his basement room at his father's house, Luke realized that he had left his cell phone at his apartment after throwing it at Brittany. Luke got the keys to his second car, a 1991 Taurus, since everyone in town knew that the tricked-out Mustang belonged to him. Luke lovingly referred to his Taurus as a "piece of crap," which might have been overly complimentary. It looked like a police car salvaged by barbarians in a Mad Max movie. Of the car's two hubcaps, one had a crack dividing it in half. There was no front bumper, and gray duct tape held the headlights in place—otherwise they would pop out and point directly at the ground. He cautiously drove the dilapidated car back to the apartment complex and parked in the rear lot.

CHAPTER 8

Mike Goodrum dated Luke's mother, Donna Goode, while they were in high school. Mike's father and grandfather were both truck drivers and his mother worked at a curtain rod factory. In 1980, after Mike graduated, he married sixteen-year-old Donna. Immediately after the ceremony, the newlyweds got into a fight on their way to the honeymoon. Mike Goodrum got out of the car, and his buddy, Bruce Dugas, picked him up in the Scottsville downtown square. Donna went on the honeymoon trip to the lake with a girlfriend. Donna gave birth to Lucas Bryan Goodrum in 1981. Donna and Mike's marriage was tumultuous and ended before Luke turned two.

Donna worked in the office at General Electric while raising Luke. There were three generations of her female kin there. Her grandmother worked in the plant, and her mother ran a router division. The women took turns babysitting Luke and traded him off in the parking lot between their shifts.

Bruce Dugas and Mike Goodrum had been good friends since high school. Bruce was known for his hard-partying ways and gambling, as well as for being a Turner. Oddly, Mike set Bruce and Donna up; Bruce had had a crush on Donna since they were teenagers at Allen County High. Bruce had just been kicked out of his parents' house when he went out with Donna. He stayed over after their first date and never left. Donna found him attractive and confident, but especially liked how he was taken with Luke. Because of his wild ways, Bruce was nicknamed "Breeze" after the untethered protagonist in the Lynyrd Skynyrd song "Call Me the Breeze." Donna's friends would tell her that she had "caught the 'Breeze.'" Their friends thought that the grounded Donna would be the anchor to finally settle Bruce down. Bruce and Donna wed on October 13, 1983.

Despite Bruce's Turner pedigree, the trappings of wealth weren't passed down to him—not yet at least. He had some shares in Dollar General, but not enough to equal a fortune. Bruce didn't work except for shooting pool at night, and Donna supported the family.

In 1985, Donna, Bruce, and Luke moved to Des Allemands, Louisiana. Bruce hunted alligators and caught crawfish for a living. Donna and Bruce had their first child, William Bruce Dugas, Jr. (known as Willie).

After she and Bruce had their own child, Donna detected a newfound schism between Bruce and Luke. She felt that Bruce's bond with Luke, which had once been paternal, was now distant. Luke was just a stepson to him.

The Dugas family returned to Scottsville in 1988. Donna and Bruce's daughter, Laura, was born in 1991. Bruce inherited money from his grandmother. Donna and Bruce's marriage problems mounted, as did Bruce's chemical habits. In July 1993, they filed for divorce. Court documents list Bruce's net worth at the time as $1,317,993.50. That autumn, when Luke was eleven, Donna filed a domestic violence petition against Bruce. It reads:

> The Petitioner says that on Sept. 12, 1993, in Allen County, Kentucky, the above named Respondent engaged in act(s) of domestic violence and abuse: He kicked in front door and broke it. Broke window. Kicked out storm door. Hit garage door with motorcycle. He has choked me and threw me around once before. The children & 2 friends were standing in bathtub hid and he came & looked at us & said we needed to talk I said no and he left.

By October, the domestic violence order had been lifted, and Bruce and Donna had gotten back together. The reunion would be short-lived, however. Two months later an incident occurred that was thereafter referred to in family lore as "Bruce's accident."

On December 29, 1993, Bruce Dugas sped around a curve on a two-lane highway in Tennessee. Bruce went into the other lane to pass and collided head-on with an oncoming car. The driver was killed instantly. Bruce tested positive for cocaine in his system. In April 1994, Dugas pleaded guilty to vehicular manslaughter and driving under the influence of a controlled substance. He was sentenced to jail.

After Bruce's incarceration, Donna moved with her children to a ranch they purchased in Aubrey, Texas. They christened it the Double D. This transition coincided with Luke's growing angst and rebellion; the more Donna disciplined him, the less he behaved. Unable to control Luke, Donna sent him to Kentucky to live with his father.

Donna wrote the following letter urging the judge to grant Bruce parole:

I am writing in regard to my husband William Bruce Dugas. He was involved in an accident and sentenced to 7 months in the Sumner County Jail. Bruce has been a model prisoner since he has been in your facility. I understand that there was a man's life taken when my husband had his accident and I also understand that there had to be a punishment. Since Bruce has been in your facility I have lost my oldest son to his natural father, he was getting out of control and there was no one here to help me with discipline, so I had to let him go live with his natural father whom he has not lived with since he was a year and a half old. His natural father really did not want to take Lucas since he has remarried and has three stepchildren. Lucas is living in a three-bedroom home. Lucas is not living in a stable environment. His natural father and step mother have a lot of problems, and the three other boys that live in the household have problems of there own. His natural father wants Lucas to come back to my home as soon as Bruce gets home . . .

Sincerely,

Donna Dugas

Bruce was released from prison, and both he and Luke returned to Texas. However, the time away hadn't improved relations between them; they were more estranged than ever. Luke was given the edict that he could either go to military school or return to live with his father. It was an easy decision. The rules and curfews were more lenient at his father's house, if not wholly nonexistent, and

Luke took advantage of the fact that his dad worked nights. Luke went out drinking and partying as much as possible.

Mike Goodrum eventually became more and more weary of Luke's difficult teenage years, which seemed to be stretching into eternity. Luke had to go. He was ordered to get all of his things out of the house and leave. He moved into an apartment with a friend.

Luke's mother had to be enlisted as a long-distance enforcer for him.

"His senior year we were in contact all the time," Donna Dugas says. "He had flunked his junior year except for one class because he didn't go to school. The guidance counselor called me on the phone and said, 'We've got to get him out of school.' I said, 'Yes, we do. What do I need to do?' She said, 'Tighten him up.' I said, 'You got it.' He made the grades and graduated and that was me keeping my foot pretty close to that butt."

CHAPTER 9

Stephen Soules was about five feet nine inches tall and skinny with tan skin. His father was black and his mother was white—he could be mistaken for various different races. A lot of his friends and family called him "Guido" because he "looked like a Mexican." The misnomer stuck.

When Stephen was younger, he had dreams of becoming a star basketball player or a famous rapper. But these adolescent reveries had dwindled down to a sluggish existence wholly in the present—a life structured around "chillin'." Stephen spent a lot of time with his buddies and cousins. They'd shoot basketball or hang out at the picnic tables at the rehab facility near his grandmother's house after it closed for the day.

Stephen's mooching could be both trying and expensive. He didn't have a car and bummed rides. He didn't have a cell phone so he always used everyone else's. Nor did he have a job or even the prospects for employment. Stephen had dropped out of high school and was now twenty years old with a ninth-grade education.

Some recall Stephen Soules as a sweet-natured polite boy, but others thought him a liar and a thief. But most anyone describing him said he was a follower. It was rarely his idea to do anything, but he could always be depended on to be the wingman.

Stephen's lack of direction often frustrated his family. But to them, Stephen's good qualities outshined the rest. Stephen was particularly devoted to his grandmother, Evangeline, whom he revered and doted upon.

On May 3, 2003, Stephen was picked up from his grandmother's house by his friend Wesley Garmon. Stephen sat in the front seat of Wesley's white Dodge Dakota, and their buddy Chris Bradshaw was in the back. Stephen and Chris Bradshaw were considered kin, not first cousins but distant relatives. The black population of Scottsville is so small that somewhere along the bloodline there is often some relation, no matter how distant. It wasn't surprising that Stephen and Chris were hanging out with a white friend, Wesley. Because of the tiny number of blacks in Scottsville, especially in the younger set, there was more of a social overlap between the races than in Bowling Green. It wasn't as rare to see young people hanging out with others of different races.

Wesley drove up Scottsville Road toward Bowling Green. Stephen was excited to get drunk and go to the frat party at the Pike House. He'd go to Western as often as he could to visit his buddies who were enrolled there and hang out at their dorms with them. Stephen was wearing a red, white, and blue sweater, dark jeans, and black Reebok sneakers. On occasion, his hair would be braided into cornrows, but mostly it was freshly barbered into a buzz cut, like today.

The boys stopped at Walmart and wandered around the aisles, killing time. After leaving, they went to Vette City Liquors and bought two eighteen-packs of Coors Light. They drove around drinking beer and listening to

music. The neighborhoods were a terrain of slight hills
and inclines. Bowling Green, like much of Kentucky, is
built upon caves, and nearby Mammoth Cave, a national
park, is the longest underground cave system in the world.
This layout can cause some structural problems, however.
The boys drove past series of houses interrupted by
sinkholes—intermittently, the earth would collapse, leaving an indented wound in the ground, with trees jutting
out like buckteeth. The hollow underground caves were
also like balloons of radon, a known carcinogen to which
many attribute the town's high cancer rates. A study
showed that 86 percent of homes with basements and 40
percent without had readings above the federally man-
dated level. The breast cancer rate is higher here than the
national average, and one group of women friends have
funerals down to a system. They rotate from funeral to
funeral; a pair of them will take turns guarding the deceased's house from robbers who might have read the
death announcement and preparing for the post-funeral
gathering. In one neighborhood, all of the mothers of a
group of childhood friends from the 1980s have since died
from the disease.

Stephen and his friends cruised past many churches.
It was impossible not to—there are over 150 in town. The
older and more traditional houses of worship—Presbyterian,
Baptist, Catholic, and Episcopal—are downtown. But outside the older quarters, a whole new breed of church has
cropped up. Some churches became an ingrained part of
the community, while others took up brief residences in
spaces such as old movie theaters. Those churches
couldn't sustain a congregation; they came and went like
comets. One church filled the lawn with row upon row of
white crosses to represent the deaths of aborted fetuses.
Another venue, big as an airplane hangar, had large

movie screens, strobe lights, baptisms in clear Plexiglas cubes, their own in-house rock band, and a modern dance troupe called "Jesus' Unwashed Feet." The church drew such large crowds that they had to build an even bigger megachurch.

Eventually the Scottsville boys tired of driving around fruitlessly and drinking beer. Chris Bradshaw called Sarah Carwell, a local girl whom he was casually dating and who had her own apartment. Sarah agreed to host them until they went to the Pike party later in the night. She wasn't surprised that Chris was bringing some buddies with him. She had learned that Scottsville boys travel in packs. Not all of them had their own car, and even if they weren't in the mood to go out, they would pile into a ride anyway for fear of missing out on something and being stranded alone for the night.

At Sarah's apartment, the boys drank beer and played with her two pit bull puppies. It wasn't long before Wesley passed out on one of the couches. After a few more beers, Stephen wanted to smoke weed. He took Wesley's cell phone and called Luke Goodrum. Luke's roommate, Matt Hire, picked up the phone. When Matt and Luke first moved in together, they both agreed that Stephen wasn't allowed over. It was widely said that after visits from Stephen, things would often turn up missing, no matter how well Stephen knew the host. Matt told Stephen that Luke wasn't there and then excitedly relayed the night's earlier drama with Brittany.

Shortly after Matt got off the phone with Stephen Soules, Luke returned to their apartment.

"Hey man, there's three cops that come in lookin' for you!" said Matt, now alone in the living room. Luke had missed them by minutes.

"Oh, shit! She did call the fuckin' po-lice!" Luke said and grabbed his cell phone.

Luke saw that he had missed a call, but he didn't recognize the number. He called it back, and Stephen answered. Luke Goodrum and Stephen's older brother, Daniel Soules, had been best friends growing up playing together in a Pee Wee football league and later on the high school basketball team. Luke and Daniel had grown apart in recent years, but they were still friendly and fond of each other. A lot of people called Daniel by his nickname, "Boonie." He was well-liked, and you would be hard-pressed to find anyone to speak ill of him.

Stephen and Luke's relationship, however, was never close. What rapport they did have revolved around marijuana. On the rare occasion when they talked on the phone, it was Stephen either trying to buy some weed or to bum some. Stephen was a frequent customer, and Luke usually gave him less product than Stephen actually paid for. When Stephen couldn't round up enough cash for a substantial amount, Luke sold him blunts for ten dollars each.

Their relationship, although shaky at best, was still leagues ahead of what it had been when they were teenagers. A few years back they had despised each other.

In high school Luke had dated the half sister of Stephen's best friend, Aaron Marr, but Marr and Luke came to blows over Luke's treatment of the girl. Then one day, Stephen wrote a note to Luke's girlfriend detailing how Luke had cheated on her. Luke discovered the letter. Later that week, Luke was cruising the strip in Glasgow and saw Stephen with some of his friends in a parking lot of a convenience store. Luke threatened to beat him up and called him "nigger" in front of the group. Stephen didn't retaliate. Luke and Stephen didn't speak to each other for a few years after this incident.

"Hey man, we heard you was in some trouble," Stephen said to Luke. Luke gave Matt a sideways glare.

"You got some weed, man?" Stephen asked. "I got some chicks over here at the crib and we ain't got no bud. We got all kinds of liquor and beer. You can come here and drink some, you need to get outta there anyway."

Stephen explained that they were having a warm-up to a frat party at Western and asked Luke to join them. The idea sounded appealing. Luke had never been to a frat party before and pictured the toga scene from *Animal House* and other college films like *Revenge of the Nerds*. It did make sense to get out of town tonight in case the police returned to his apartment.

Stephen tried to tell Luke how to get to Sarah's, but Luke didn't know his way around Bowling Green. Luke told him to just pick him up in the parking lot of Southern Lanes bowling alley near the mall.

Luke returned to his father's house to switch cars again, fearing that the decrepit Taurus wouldn't survive the short trek to Bowling Green. The Mustang started with a roar and he cautiously made his way through back roads to the entrance of I-65. The highway takes about as long as Scottsville Road, but Luke figured there would be fewer police. He pulled onto the entrance ramp and the red taillights moved into the distance before merging with the others, gradually getting smaller and smaller until they disappeared.

Sarah drove Stephen to Southern Lanes in her maroon Honda to meet Luke, but he hadn't arrived yet. Soon Luke pulled into the lot, the silver Mustang's engine so loud it sounded like a crew of workmen jackhammering, a construction site on wheels. Luke was going fast, and he cut rapidly so the tires shrieked as he slid into the space in front of Sarah's car.

Luke hopped out of his car, strutted over, his chin uplifted, and got into the backseat.

"Hey, we goin' to that frat party?" he asked excitedly without bothering to introduce himself to Sarah.

On the way back to Sarah's apartment, Luke unfurled more details of the evening's earlier Brittany fiasco, rounding out his tale with, "I'm ready to party, man. Fuck that girl, man."

The Scottsville crew drank more beer and brandy and passed around two blunts that Luke supplied, except for Wesley, who was still in a coma-thick inebriated slumber. Luke didn't feel like drinking, though, and held off. Stephen drank about twelve beers by himself. *Rocky IV* played on the television and the Philly hero was fighting off the Russian interloper.

Two Scottsville buddies, Damian Secrest and Brian Moon, soon arrived to pick up the crew to go to the frat party. They had been out in the country at a high school prom party.

"C'mon man, we got beer here," Chris Bradshaw said to Luke and Stephen. He was trying to talk them into just staying at Sarah's with them.

But they had no intention of remaining. Stephen wanted some excitement, and Luke was curious to check out a frat party. Luke and Stephen piled into Brian Moon's maroon Ford truck with the shiny silver corrugated-metal toolbox in the back.

CHAPTER 10

Katie and Danica were drinking "Golden Grain," a dirt-cheap, 190-proof pure grain alcohol, mixed with Sierra Mist lemon-lime soda. They were down the hall in room 211 with Danica's ex-roommate, Amy Nussmeier, and one of her friends who was visiting from Louisville. Early in the first semester Nussmeier and Danica had been quite close, but the two started having problems, stopped speaking, and eventually stopped living together. They had started socializing again, little by little, about a month before, and tonight was the first time Amy had ever hung out with Katie, the girl who had replaced her in 214.

This was just the preface to tonight's real event: a fraternity party at Pi Kappa Alpha, commonly referred to as Pike House. Katie was excited for something to do, especially since a lot of their friends had gone to Louisville for the Derby.

After an hour or so and a few drinks, Nussmeier dropped Danica and Katie off at the Pike House. It was around midnight. The frat house was a quaint two-story stone dwelling whose attractive exterior belied a mess inside.

"It is *gross*," Danica said to Katie. "These boys don't ever clean. It smells."

All of the furniture was moved into one room. About 250 people had come to the party that night, and around seventy remained, a moderate turnout, since so many students were in Louisville for Derby weekend. A DJ played commercial hip-hop and one of the cleared-out rooms was used as a makeshift dance floor.

Katie was extremely intoxicated. Danica could handle her liquor, but Katie was clumsy when it came to such rites. She didn't know her limits and her tolerance was extremely low. She would be drinking and suddenly intoxication would wash over her but she wouldn't stop, even if Danica tried to get the alcohol away from her (which she always tried to do). The alcohol often unleashed pent-up emotions. Katie was frequently teary; her enormous, ever-present smile would crumble away and all the pain she had inside would seep out.

Katie had not gotten to that point yet, but as the minutes ticked by she became more incoherent. She wore a burgundy shirt and dark blue jeans with black high heels. She carried a purse that was woven like a basket and had brown leather handles. Both her and Danica's cell phones were in her handbag, which was the usual protocol. Katie would always carry a purse, and Danica preferred to toss her makeup and other debris into Katie's bag than lug one around all night.

"She kept running all over the place," Danica says. "You couldn't keep up with her. One minute she's over here, the next minute she's over there. So, I basically stood in one spot and watched her come in and out of the room. She just kind of got out of control. I guess when you've got a small group that knows each other and she's out of control obviously drawing attention to herself, it was like, 'Who's this drunk girl? What is wrong with her?' "

The half case of beer, the marijuana, and the brandy caught up with Stephen during the ride to the Pike House. He had been drinking on an empty stomach, and the bumping motion of the truck didn't help matters, nor did being crammed into the small cab with the other guys. Damian parked and Brian grabbed a bottle of tequila from underneath the seat. Damian, Brian, and Luke got out, leaving Stephen to convalesce in the vehicle. Stephen asked them to leave the air conditioner on, but they didn't want to run the battery down. Stephen leaned over, vomited on the floorboard, set his head against the cool glass of the passenger's side window, and passed out. Fuzzy black dice dangled from the rearview mirror like mistletoe.

The other boys walked around the stone house to the patio and sat down. The party did not live up to Luke's toga-and-keg fantasies. It was not beer-fueled mayhem but seemed to be mostly groups of preppy university students who already knew one another. The party was a "senior send-off" for a Pike who was leaving for dental school, not that Luke and his friends were aware of this, nor would they have cared if they were.

The boys saw Ryan Payne, a Pike pledge whom they went to high school with, and who had been a football teammate of Luke. Most everyone referred to Payne as Possum. Possum was a hulking young man, six-two and heavyset, weighing 240 pounds. He moved and talked as slowly as his namesake. Possum's hair was bleached a blondish yellow and he had on a white-and-blue checkered shirt. Possum and his fellow initiates were designated sober drivers for the night and had to keep an eye on the house.

Katie called Maurice numerous times to tell him to come to the party and he finally arrived with his roommate. He told Katie that she couldn't stay with him that night. The next day he had plans to play football with his friends and his parents were also coming for a visit. Katie asked him to dance, but he declined. As always, he knew a lot of people at the party, and he just didn't feel like dealing with her in the condition she was in.

"I'm going to walk around real quick and then I'll come back and dance with you," he told her.

When Maurice didn't return from his detour, Katie sought him out.

"Forget you! I hate you!" Katie screamed and slapped him hard in the face. Her emotions, already turgid and confused from the drinking, boiled over and she started bawling.

The altercation didn't go unnoticed by the other partygoers. Possum walked over and asked what was wrong. Through her tears, Katie said she would be fine. She walked outside with Maurice following her. She told him she hated him but both of them knew that was far from the truth.

Outside the party, Stephen was still passed out in the truck when Luke shook him awake.

"Damn, man, the police is outside! Straighten up!" Luke said.

Stephen didn't have it in him to feign sobriety yet. He muttered to Luke to calm down, that the police often cruise by campus parties to make sure nothing is out of hand and that it was no big deal. Luke returned to the party and Stephen went straight back to sleep.

He awoke a short time later. After Wesley had passed out at Sarah's, Stephen had taken his cell phone to use for the night. It wasn't as if Wesley was going to use it any-way, he reassured himself. At 12:58 AM Stephen called a high school friend, Brian Richey, who lived in Bowling Green. When Richey realized who was on the line, he knew that Stephen would be asking for something. Sure enough, Stephen asked Brian to come pick him up from the party. Richey told him that he couldn't give him a ride because he had to be up at 7 AM. Stephen called again later, but Richey didn't bother answering.

Up until he saw Katie, security guard Josh Mills had bus-ied himself either stopping the partygoers from drinking on the front porch or breaking up fights in the backyard. "The party was going fine," Mills later said in a report, "until I seen a short blonde-headed young teenage girl dancing in a very aggressive manner with a couple of black males. She was throwing her pelvis into their private area."

Katie dropped her purse and everything spilled out of it—the cell phones, her compact, and other items were strewn across the dance floor.

"Is this purse yours?" Mills asked Katie. He stooped over, put the scattered items back into the bag, and tried to hand it to her. Katie kept dancing as if he weren't there.

Katie walked past the Scottsville boys standing by the dance floor. She skimmed her hand across Luke's stom-ach as she passed him on the way to the bathroom. She was soon dancing with Chris Bradshaw and Damian and some other guys. Luke stayed on the sidelines surveying the party.

Katie's behavior came to the attention of security again. "She was dancing with some male subjects that came in with other females," Mills said, "and those other females either got jealous or upset that Katie was dancing with their friends. Katie was giving the middle finger to the other white females. They was just giving each other the middle finger back and forth. She was just there dancing with literally every guy on the dance floor. Each time I looked at Katie, she was dancing with a different guy. And she was walking across the dance floor and bumped into a white girl and made her drop her beer. They started cussing each other. And Katie as she walked away she was still cussing."

Katie's behavior was out of character, contrasting with her usually meek public demeanor. The Pike members had now had enough of Katie, and asked security to remove her. When Katie reconvened with Danica, she was tearful, slurring, and making little sense.

"They're making me leave!" Katie wailed to Danica.

Danica told the guard that she would take Katie out of the party. "We came together and we'll leave together," she said.

A pledge came up to Danica and volunteered to take Katie home. It was Ryan "Possum" Payne.

The girls went outside to try to arrange a departure. Minutes later, Mills walked out and saw that they were still there. "The white girl was very upset," he stated. "She was crying. She had tears coming down her face and there was several, two black males and I believe three white males standing around the black girl and the white girl. The black girl was hugging the white girl as if she was trying to comfort her in some way."

"You need to leave. You're still on the property," Mills said to the girls.

"The black girl made a statement that she just broke up with her boyfriend," Mills remembered, "and that everybody goes through this and she'd be all right. 'She needs some time to herself. Let her be by herself.' The black girl didn't appear to be intoxicated at all. She had no type of signs of being under the influence and was mostly taking up for the white girl. She wouldn't let any guys close to her."

Some of the other revelers snickered and made fun of Katie.

"She's leavin'! She's drunk. What the hell is your problem? Shut up!" Danica said as she marched toward the hecklers. "If anybody fucks with my friend I'm goin' to fuck 'em up!"

"I'm ridin' with Ryan, I'm ridin' with Ryan," Katie kept muttering. Possum soon appeared and stood next to her.

Brian Moon had agreed to lend Possum his truck, complete with the passed-out Stephen Soules. After Possum finished his rounds ferrying drunk revelers, he could then leave the truck at Bemis Lawrence Hall, Brian's dorm. Moon wasn't in a condition to drive, so it worked out well to have his truck driven home for him. The plan was for Brian, Damian, and Luke to walk to Bemis Lawrence, where Stephen would be waiting for them after Possum dropped him off.

Earlier in the night, Danica had met a boy who she thought was cute. He invited her back to his apartment for a small after-party, and Danica decided to go with him. "I wouldn't leave her somewhere," Danica says of Katie. "I knew how naïve she could be. She was very small, and I was a little bit more street smart than she was and so I was really uneasy about leaving her with somebody in the first place. But I had kind of gotten to the point where I was so tired of babysitting her all the time. I was always looking out for her. And so it was like, 'Okay, I'm going here, they're gonna take you home.' "

"If anybody touches Katie, I'm gonna hurt somebody," Danica told Possum. Danica gave her a hug, and Katie walked over to the maroon pickup with Possum. Stephen Soules was still slumped inside.

When the driver's side door of the truck opened and the overhead light came on, the sound and glare pierced Stephen's slumber. Stephen raised up from his hunched-over position and saw Possum get behind the wheel.

The rest had done Stephen well and he felt better. By this time he had also expunged most of the alcohol in his system. "I done puked so much I couldn't puke no more," he recalled. Luckily, the smell wasn't too bad, since it was basically pure alcohol that came up as Stephen hadn't eaten before going out.

Katie, still weepy, got in and Stephen scooted over. She was disheveled from the night's odyssey but still radiant, crying, and fragile. The small cabin was crowded with the trio. The three youths were lined up in ascending order of size: from tiny Katie to lanky Stephen to imposing Possum.

The truck drove away. Still bothered by the uneasy feeling that had been mounting all day, Danica stored the last four digits of the truck's license plate number in her phone, which she had retrieved from Katie's purse, just in case something happened.

Hugh Poland Hall is only a two-minute drive from the Pike House. The parking lot was a vast dark sea. Katie got out and began lurching up the shadowed concrete path, and Possum puttered away.

Stephen said to him, "I'm gonna go back and holler at her."

The police broke up the party, and Brian, Damian, and Luke walked to Bemis Lawrence. It was a nice night and it was only about a ten-minute journey if they cut across lawns.

Luke told the guys that he wanted to sell his Mustang and asked if they would be interested—they weren't. Brian signed Damian into the hall as a guest. Luke sat on a couch while Damian and Brian chatted with Londa, the RA (residential advisor) on front desk duty, whom they were chummy with. She noted 2:15 as their arrival time on the sheet. Despite the late hour, the boys seemed to Londa to be in good condition and sober. Luke struck her as being extremely quiet. They asked her if she had seen Stephen, since he was driving and should have beaten them there. Londa and Stephen had met the weekend before when he had come by with Damian. But, no, she hadn't seen him that night at all. She thought that Luke was "nice looking" and she asked Damian who he was.

"He didn't talk," Londa says of Luke. "He was just quiet. Most people that come in that are drinking and everything, they're like loud and obnoxious and want to talk and everything, and they're bouncing everywhere. He just sat down and didn't do anything. He wasn't at all loud."

At 2:18 AM, Damian called Possum to remind him to pick up Luke. Possum told him that he still had to give some people rides back to their dorms and that he'd collect Luke as soon as he could. A Domino's deliverywoman came by with an order for one of the residents. Moon half jokingly tried to buy the pizza from her. About twenty minutes later, Possum showed up and Luke went out and got into the truck with him.

En route to the bowling alley, the two discussed how this was the first time they had seen each other since high school. Luke tried to push the Mustang on Possum, too. When they got to Southern Lanes, Luke went so far as to start the engine so Possum could hear the roar. Possum said he would get back to him about it even though he really had no intention of buying it. Possum left and Luke went around the corner of the building and urinated against the brown brick wall.

After the Pike party, Danica went with the boys to McDonald's and then on to their apartment.

"Katie should have called me by now," Danica thought. "Something's wrong. Something's wrong."

When she voiced her concerns, the resounding response was, "She's fine, she's probably just passed out."

Danica tried to push it out of her mind. She and another girl were at the apartment; they were laughing and dancing and the guys continued drinking. Danica received a few phone calls from some friends who had gone to Louisville for the Derby to tell her about the festivities. One of them was from near Pellville, and it reminded Danica to check up on Katie. She tried Katie's cell phone and their dorm line but didn't get a response. Finally, Katie answered at 2:26 AM. It sounded like she was lying facedown into her pillow.

"Are you okay? Did you make it up okay?"

"Yeah."

In the background, Danica heard their door shut.

"Danica, I'm scared, someone just came into the room," Katie said.

"Well, who is it?"

"I don't know. I don't know."

"Well, get up and look and tell me who it is."

"Danica, I don't know. I don't know who it is," Katie slurred. Her voice sounded muffled.

"Put them on the phone."

Danica heard a male's voice and she asked him who he was.

"I'm the boy who brought her home. She got sick in my truck and so I just wanted to make sure she was okay."

Danica told him to turn Katie on her side in case she vomited. Danica thought that she heard another male voice in the background and the door close.

Katie took the phone again and mumbled, "I just wanna go to sleep. I just wanna go to sleep."

A little after 2:28 AM, the call ended. Danica phoned Amy Nussmeier down the hall to see if she could check on Katie. Danica was concerned, but not overly worried— she thought Katie was "just being drunk." The call went to Amy's voice mail.

CHAPTER 11

Officer Raphael Casas of the WKU police was dispatched to investigate the fire alarm that sounded at 4:08 AM at Hugh Poland Hall. Upon his arrival on the second floor, he saw water seeping out from beneath the door to room 214. Casas unlocked the door with his master key and opened it. Black smoke billowed in his face and he slammed the door shut. He ran to the floor's bathroom and wet a paper towel to use as a makeshift breathing mask. While Casas was on his way back to the room, the shift commander radioed and told him not to enter, to exit the building altogether, and wait for the Bowling Green Fire Department, which was on the way.

The BGFD gets a lot of calls to Western's dorms, usually involving burnt food in the shared kitchens, pranksters pulling the alarms, or faulty smoke detectors. Engine #5 pulled into the parking lot at 4:14 AM. Three more trucks were following. Captain Bob Sanborn was in charge of #5's crew. Dorm alarms like this were pretty routine and usually amounted to nothing.

"Ninety-five percent of the time the sprinklers put them out," Sanborn explains. "You call it half-stepping. You do everything procedure-wise. You wouldn't think someone would be in there. Fires in dorm rooms, you simply go up and open the door, 'Yeah, the sprinkler put it out.' Shut the sprinkler down. It's all salvage stuff. Overhaul."

Sanborn continues, "We knew all those buildings were sprinklered. Usually the cops are there on the scene, and they were. And they reported an actual fire, but I'm thinking, Okay, I'm still cool. Fire's going to be contained in that room."

It takes training and experience not to treat these situations with complacency, and Sanborn lacked neither. In his fifties, Sanborn was nearing retirement, but he was physically capable of any job at hand. His arms were sinewy, veined and muscled; his knowing eyes were framed by bushy gray brows that matched an ample mustache.

Sanborn and firefighter Matt Jones went to the second floor and put their masks on in the stairwell before entering the hallway. Light smoke draped the air. The steady stream of water was still coming from underneath the door. Sanborn opened it and saw that the fire was out but the room was filled with "cold smoke," black clouds of smoke from an extinguished fire. Water spewed from the overhead sprinkler. The water piercing the black clouds looked like a hellish storm pouring brimstone rain. The sun still hadn't risen yet, and no light came through the window. The room was impenetrably black; the small space became subterranean, cavernous, and endless.

Sanborn turned and instructed Jones, "Go ahead and start the primary search. Make sure we don't have anyone in the hallways."

Sanborn stared into the black and saw something glistening on one of the beds. The overhead fluorescent lights from the hallway reflected on something, causing a slight shine to slice the blackness, like the glow of some bioluminescent fish barely visible in the depths of the sea. The breathing from Sanborn's mask was audible. A stalactite mass hung overhead, and Sanborn assumed it was part of the ceiling sagging down. In actuality it was Katie's afghan, wrapped around the gushing sprinkler spigot. The smoke detector hung from its wires.

Sanborn cautiously stepped inside and the door closed behind him. He tried to adjust to the blackness that consumed him, blindly inching toward the bed, which he could now see was covered in a smoldering pile of blankets and clothes. His eyes focused. He saw that the glistening was a patch of exposed flesh, the skin burnt off an arm protruding from the pyrelike mound.

"I brushed back the burning stuff," Sanborn says, "this smoldering mess. At the time I didn't know if it was a female or a male. But what I did notice immediately was the face was wrapped real tight and the nose was pressed down with some type of sheer cloth, like someone was trying to play a game, like a Halloween costume, like robbers when the nylon contorts the face." A white T-shirt was knotted tightly around Katie Autry's neck and the remnants of the turquoise T-shirt that Maurice gave her, the shirt that she lovingly slept in each night, clung to her shoulders.

Sanborn loudly blurted out, "What in the hell?! What are you doing here?"

He saw Katie's chest rise and fall. He was shocked to see signs of life.

"I got a victim! I need help!" Sanborn shouted into the radio.

He scooped Katie up and wrapped her in the charred, wet sheet. "She was very slippery," Sanborn recalls. "At best she was 110 pounds. And what I didn't do is 'scotch' the door, put a wedge underneath the door. As I'm trying to open the door she slips a little bit and she was sliding down and right about when I got my foot by the door and I got her out in the hallway and I looked at the enormity of the situation and she was just terribly burned."

Sanborn swung open the door carrying Katie just as Sergeants Jerry Bridgeman and Bryan Fulkerson got to the second floor. They took over evacuating her.

"We were just holding the corners up," Bridgeman remembers. "The victim was cocooned inside the sheet. I was leading and we were starting to head down the stairwell. The stairwell was slippery. There was water pouring down and I was having to hold on to the sheet with one hand and kind of guide myself along the handrail with the other hand to keep from falling. I've got all my gear on, and I remember thinking, This has got to be a joke or something, because whoever it is I'm carrying doesn't weigh anything. I'm holding her with one hand.

"Once we got her down to the ground floor," Bridgeman continues, "I was able to let go of the stairwell. I grabbed the sheet with my other hand. I had both hands on the sheet as we backed out the door and I opened up the sheet just to grab the corners, not necessarily to look at whoever it was. But still in my head I was thinking, This can't be a real person because there's just not enough weight here. When I opened it up I saw that it was somebody."

The firefighters ripped off their helmets, tilted their heads skyward, and called out, "Medic! Medic! Need a medic!" but there were none to answer their calls.

"Get some air going on her off your mask!" Sanborn barked to his men, thinking that Katie hadn't succumbed to smoke inhalation because the cloth tied around her face had acted as a filter.

When the ambulance pulled up, the firefighters were still helping Katie breathe. "She was actually fighting the

O$_2$ mask that we put on her face," Fulkerson says, "just taking her hand and trying to remove it, just knocking it off her face. We got some packs that got burn gel in it, but they're pretty small, they're not for major burns. So pretty much at this time we're just trying to find something sterile to get her covered up with and by the time we even really started looking for it that's when the ambulance showed up and they kind of walked there, so they took pretty much over at that point."

"There was a delay because the police dispatch didn't have the volume turned up," says one of the first responders. He alleges that the dispatcher's radio had been turned down to an inaudible level after the initial report that there were no victims and that this was why there wasn't an ambulance there waiting and why the medics didn't comprehend the gravity of the situation upon their arrival. "Everyone was thinking it's a student with a stubbed toe," he says, "not that someone had been horribly burned."

The EMS crew loaded Katie onto a gurney and hurried her into the ambulance. Sergeant Fulkerson rode with her to the Medical Center. The paramedic tried to get an IV inserted into her arm, the glistening arm that silently signaled her presence, but it was difficult because of the burn damage.

"Just take me home," Katie muttered as she limply tried to swat the mask from her face. The damage to her larynx reduced her high voice to a squawk.

"Just take me home," she repeated and vainly tried to remove the oxygen mask again.

It was now officially Mother's Day, and despite the early hour, Katie's mother, Donnie Autry, was awake. In hindsight, she sees this as "mother's intuition." Donnie and her boyfriend were in Bowling Green spending the weekend at his mother's house. She had stayed up into the early morning hours listening to their new distraction, a police scanner.

Donnie heard "Hugh Poland" crackling through the speaker numerous times. She had been there before to visit Katie, just a few days earlier, in fact. On Thursday, they had met there before going to McDonald's.

Donnie called Katie's dorm phone, but no one responded. Police were doing a preliminary search of the dorm room. Some items had been washed into the hall by the cascading water: a bandanna and a purple can of Aussie hair spray. The hair spray was Katie's, but she never used it. It had been stored behind the toiletries that she did use. Scraps of the sheet used to carry Katie out were strewn about the linoleum floor.

When Katie was wheeled into the emergency room, she was covered in third-degree burns so thick that her skin was as hard as wood, and her body was still smoking. She was moaning and still trying to push the mask away from her face.

"The extent of her burns—if you can call it a blessing, there was probably very little pain involved at that point," says Emily Barton, one of the attending techs. "Because once you get to third-degree burns, which were most of hers, the burn has killed away nerves so there's not very much pain. She had some minor burns elsewhere that might have been painful. By definition she was conscious because she was moaning and making a purposeful movement. Whether I think she realized what was going on, no."

Barton continues, "We get her in the bed, and one of the very first things that we notice is that she has a T-shirt knotted around her neck. She had obvious bruising on her face, almost an indention on the left side of her face. She had a black eye. The other thing that we noticed was her burn pattern. She had no burns on her back or her legs, it was all on the front and it was from just about the top of her breasts down to probably mid-thigh, groin area. People that fall asleep on the couch smoking a cigarette and catch on fire, they have burns on the back. If you fall asleep on the bed and your mattress catches on fire, you really should have burns on your back. There's no burns on her back, no burns on her legs. She should have circumventral burns which go all the way around the extremities, her trunk and that type of stuff, and she did not have that."

"Get the police here! This is not an accident!" yelled the team leader, Dr. Lee Carter. Also noticeable were two puncture wounds on Katie's neck. Her eye was bruised and swollen shut.

The techs put paper bags on Katie's hands in an effort to preserve what evidence they could. They bagged the clothes, cutting away the T-shirt tied around her neck. Katie's toenails were polished a silvery blue, and a thin ring was around one of her toes. Her belly-button ring was melted into her skin. A breathing tube was inserted down Katie's swollen throat. Dr. Carter was soon on the phone trying to get her transferred to the burn unit at Vanderbilt University in Nashville. The Medical Center was not equipped to handle burns of Katie's magnitude, and a helicopter was dispatched to collect her. The staff was putting sterile cool water and towels on Katie, trying to cover her from infection, and tried to insert a catheter.

"We put in a Foley catheter because normally when you have a severe burn, your kidneys shut down because your blood literally boils underneath the skin and then that shuts your kidneys down," says Carter.

"It was very difficult with her burns," says Barton. "There

is a specific spot you go, it's called the urinary miatus, and that's basically the opening where your urine comes out. The problem with this particular thing was that was all burned off. So basically there was no opening that you could very well distinguish, we were just basically guessing to where it should have been."

The ER team was working in a state of high tension and extreme frustration.

"Before the first law enforcement officer got there," says Barton, "the helicopter was already there and we had been on the phone demanding somebody from any law enforcement office to come because we knew that this was not an accident and that this was going to be a homicide investigation. Typically police come and take pictures and that type of stuff. We had a hard time getting law enforcement there. We called everybody. We called Western, we called the city, we called the county, we called the state, just trying to get anybody. Right as the helicopter was landing, I think a state trooper had shown up and took several pictures. Then we loaded her up and she was flown to Vanderbilt. We were not holding up her transport for anything and as far as we were concerned they could get in their vehicle and drive down there."

When Katie was taken to the helicopter, she left a charged emotional ambience in her wake.

"Everybody was in shell shock," Barton says. "Dr. Carter is the most even-keeled person you could ever meet, basically, one mode: he's always nice. He's just very stoic. He doesn't get angry."

Dr. Carter picked up a chair and hurled it across the room.

In Morgantown, away from the commotion about thirty minutes south in Bowling Green, the White family was asleep. Katie's cousin, Barbie, was dozing lightly in the living room.

Katie's foster mother, Shirley Inman, called at approximately 5:20 AM.

"I was on the couch half awake and half asleep," Barbie says. "My uncle had done called like four times, so I was just like kinda in and out. The phone started ringing and I just assumed it was him again and I wasn't gonna get up and answer it. And then the answering machine picked up and I heard Shirley crying."

Shirley Inman told her that Katie was in the hospital. Barbie ran and woke up her parents and handed the phone to her mother, Katie's aunt, Virginia.

After the frantic call from Shirley Inman, Virginia phoned the Medical Center. She was told that Katie's condition was critical and that she was going to be taken to the burn unit at Vanderbilt University in Nashville.

Ten minutes later, Virginia was speeding down the highway with her husband, Johnny, and Barbie. She drove with one hand on the steering wheel and the other punching keys on her cell phone. Virginia was calling friends and relatives and asking them to pray.

Amy Nussmeier called Danica to tell her about the fire. She told Danica that smoke was coming from her room.

"Oh, great," Danica said, thinking Katie drunkenly kicked over one of her candles. "She's gone and burnt down our damn room. Great."

Danica had the flaw of youth, the illusion of invulnerability. They were young and strong, nothing would ever happen to them. She asked Amy where Katie was, and Amy didn't know. Danica told her to go find out what was going on and to call her back. Danica called her mother.

She done lost everything, whatever, Mrs. Jackson thought.

About twenty minutes later, Amy called Danica and told her what she had heard: that Katie had been pulled from the building and was blackened by smoke, but was breathing. The gravity of the situation still didn't sink in.

Everyone at the apartment was drunk, and Danica was stranded without a ride. She finally found two friends to come pick her up. When Danica got to the dorm, the police approached her.

"They pretty much immediately take me off to the station," Danica says, "and I'm wondering, Why are they questioning me about certain things? I thought, Okay, they said she's at the hospital, she probably just has smoke inhalation. And then they started asking me all these weird questions like, 'Were there scissors out? Did you have knives in the room?' Finally, they were like, 'She has puncture wounds.' And that was the first time I thought somebody did this to her. They kept asking me was she suicidal. I was like, 'No!' Then little by little, it was like, 'Oh, she had burns. Oh she had third-degree burns. Oh, well, they're covering her body.'"

CHAPTER 12

Katie's best guy friend, Jason Allen, arrived back at his dorm from spending the night out with a friend. Hugh Poland Hall was surrounded by police cars and fire engines. The entrances were cordoned off with police tape. Allen, a tall pharmacy student, was one of the first people Katie had met at college. After exchanging glances for several days, Jason introduced himself after an orientation luncheon and they learned that they were both in Poland Hall. Katie and Jason became inseparable as the summer segued into the school year, their platonic relationship built upon a thinly shielded mutual crush.

As time progressed, Jason and Katie's friendship became closer. "If we ever had something going on," Jason says, "we could talk to each other. There is no words to describe how awesome she was. If I needed her she was there. I would call her and she would be up in my room immediately. She would drop whatever it was she was doing. I think we clicked from the get-go. I'm not a devout Christian as far as going to church every week and everything but I am a Christian and it seemed that she was the same way."

Jason and Katie shared an 8 AM class, a tedious required course for freshmen that taught them things such as how to use the library and familiarize themselves with the campus. The pair would meet in the lobby and walk to class together. They'd get a coffee if they had the time. They would skip when they could get away with it since roll wasn't taken. At night, Katie and Jason would go bowling at the student center or party-hop around campus since they couldn't get into the bars.

"Eventually, I did grow an attraction to her," Jason says, "and her to me. She would color me pictures in a coloring book and leave them under my door. We would talk for hours about anything and everything. There was never one time that she wasn't willing to be there or help. She was just so nice and genuine—always thanking somebody. My window would be open in my dorm room and she'd yell my name and ask to come up."

Katie and Jason became more than just friends, but were not officially boyfriend and girlfriend. It was a time of adjustment, and neither was necessarily looking to settle down with the other, or at least voice it if they were. Whatever it is that they had together, though, created the awkwardness of not really wanting the other party to know about one's other romantic predicaments.

As school progressed, the degree of difficulty augmented for Katie. The work was harder than in high school, and there were all the social distractions that she had never encountered before. "She did fairly well in the first semester," Jason says, "but in the second when anatomy and things get a little harder she was having some trouble. That's when it seems like she would ask me for more help. That's when it seems like she would get down. Sometimes she would mention her dad or mom. She would mention how sometimes she felt like she might be letting them down."

The following is an undated letter from Katie Autry to her birth mother, Donnie Autry:

Mom,

Hey how are ya? I'm pretty good. We are getting ready to go to Louisville, I just thought I'd write ya a little note before I go. Not much is going on right now, nothing interesting anyway. Classes are alright, I'm gonna try to do better it's just too easy to skip & sleep in then get drunk & mess around. I want to do better & be good, I'm just not used to being able to do my own thing & be my own person. I was too sheltered back home. I'm just experiencing all of these new things which is cool, but a little overwhelming. I am gonna try to get my act together, though. Well, I better be going. I love you & I'll talk to ya later.

Love,

Katie

CHAPTER 13

When Katie arrived at Vanderbilt, she was sedated and connected to a mechanical ventilator. Her blood pressure was low and she underwent additional resuscitation. A doctor cut long slits in Katie's skin, a procedure called an escharotomy, so Katie's chest could rise and fall when she breathed, as her epidermis was too toughened by the fire to do so otherwise. The doctors excised the burns and replaced the skin with grafts from a cadaver. At approximately 10 AM her condition was listed as being "extremely critical." An hour later it worsened to "severely critical."

The Whites met the Inmans at the Medical Center in Bowling Green. Virginia's husband, Johnny, returned to Morgantown to fetch their youngest daughter, Lil' Johnni. Virginia, Barbie, and Donnie drove to Nashville with Jim and Shirley Inman. This would be one of the last instances of solidarity between Katie's blood and foster families.

The Inmans and the Autrys were as different as could be, and they had scraped against one another like tectonic plates for years. Katie and Lisa visited Aunt Virginia on holidays and enjoyed having a more lax set of rules.

"I was under the impression that the Inmans could

stop the visits," Virginia says. "At one point I was threatened with that. The girls had been up for a visit. Shirley called me and told me if those girls come back with an attitude again like they did this time I would not be allowed any more visits. I don't know what she was talking about. She asked me, 'Did anything happen?' And I said, 'Not to my knowledge. When they left my house they were fine. I could not see no attitude.'"

The one time Barbie went to stay at the Inmans' for a weekend, Katie was grounded. Therefore, Barbie was grounded for her visit, too.

Once at Vanderbilt, relations between the households immediately started to deteriorate.

"The Inmans and I did not see eye to eye at the hospital on quite a few things," Virginia says. "Right off of the bat, we had to sit out in the waiting area and when they come out to tell us how Katie was doing, they asked for the parents. The Inmans were *not* Katie's parents."

"My opinion," Virginia continues: "Katie would not have wanted them making her final decisions. The more I tried to get a say in it, the bigger fight I got from them."

In a rare statement, Jim Inman told the WKU student newspaper, the *College Heights Herald,* "We think the world of Katie. I don't know what else I can say other than that we are very concerned and that she is in our prayers."

When Virginia was allowed to see Katie, despite being forewarned, she wasn't prepared for the actuality.

"They took us back there," Virginia remembers, "and the nurses were saying that she wasn't cleaned up or anything. And I said, 'That was okay, I still wanted to see her.' And I went in there and I went into hysterics."

Adding to the turmoil at the burn unit would be the arrival of two new visitors, Danica and her mother.

"My thought was," Donna Jackson recalls, "Danica can

get Katie to wake up if she's unconscious. I believed that. I honestly thought that if we get there, and if Danica gets to see Katie, she can say, 'Come on! Come on!' I know that Danica felt the same way."

Lisa had met Danica before when she visited Katie at Western. Lisa wasn't particularly taken with Danica, finding her more aggressive than Katie's Pellville friends. The three girls hung out in the room, and then went to an on-campus concert to see Nappy Roots, a local rap group that had become a national success. After a few songs the girls left the show to go to frat parties. Katie was in her "mother hen" mode and didn't drink around Lisa, nor did she let Lisa indulge.

Donna Jackson described the scene at the hospital: "Well, we get there, and we see Katie's aunt. She's a steely-eyed bitch, let me tell you. She's mean-looking to begin with. From the time we got there, she was giving Danica all kinds of dirty looks and rolling her eyes. I don't know what her problem was, I never could understand that."

"She asked how Katie was doing," Virginia said of Danica, "and I told her it was critical and I asked her, 'What happened? Y'all were always together? What happened?' If I ever receive a phone call like that from my best friend telling me someone's in the room . . . Granted, I don't know what her condition was or what her thinkin' was at that point. I don't know what went through her mind."

Danica and her mother left the hospital and drove back to Bowling Green. "We weren't wanted there," Donna Jackson says. "It was like the aunt thought that Danica had something to do with it from the very beginning. That was what kept running through my mind: Do they think that Danica had something to do with this?"

CHAPTER 14

The morning of the fire, Brian Richey woke up at 7 AM. It was going to be a very busy Sunday. He and his girlfriend, Mary, had stayed up late the night before, packing for their impending move to a new house. And today he was going to help her out in her job with the housing authority—they were taking a group of senior citizens on a fishing trip.

Brian shuffled into the living room to have a cigarette. The apartment was in the midst of being dismantled. He went over to the sofa and inadvertently sat on Stephen Soules, who was sleeping soundly, camouflaged by a blanket covering him head to toe. Richey leapt up in shock.

"How the hell did you get here?" Brian asked him incredulously. He immediately wondered if Stephen was hiding to stay at the house after he left.

Stephen told him that he had walked from the party. Brian found this ludicrous, since he considered Stephen much too lazy to walk all the way from Western to his house, especially after a late night of partying. Brian had no time for Stephen to be bumming a ride on a day like this. And he was unhappy with Stephen for letting himself in without even knocking. Disrespectful, plain and simple. Brian muttered some curses and walked into the other room. He told Stephen that he couldn't take him to Scottsville, that he and Mary had to take some elderly people fishing. Stephen asked for a lift to Sarah Carwell's over near Bowling Green High. Grudgingly, Brian acquiesced. He didn't really have any choice and had to get rid of him.

Brian and his girlfriend loaded their two Chesapeake Bay retrievers into the back of his pickup truck so they could drop them off in the pen at their new place. As he backed out of the driveway, Brian didn't notice the purple child's bicycle lying in his front yard.

They pulled up to Sarah's and saw that Wesley's truck was still outside. Stephen went to the front door and banged on it until, after a while, Chris Bradshaw groggily appeared and let him in. Bradshaw asked Stephen how the party was, and he replied that he spent the evening in the truck being sick. They woke up Wesley so that he could drive them all home.

The twenty-minute ride back to Scottsville was mostly silent. All three had had a rough night of drinking. As they entered Scottsville, the billboard with five of the Ten Commandments, many of which had been broken the night previously, loomed from the steep hill. Wesley dropped Stephen off at his grandmother's house. Stephen ostensibly lived at his father's house, but he mostly slept on the couch at his grandmother's.

Evangeline, or "Vangie," Soules lived in a tiny, brownish-yellow wood-framed house. The little cottage only had room for a door and a single window on the façade. In the lot next door was the weathered concrete foundation for a house that hadn't bothered to get built. It was as if something had spooked the builders and they had had a change of heart, or else a tornado had selectively plucked a house from its lot.

Evangeline's house was in a traditionally black neighborhood of Scottsville. The quarter's unofficial sobriquet, Boxtown, was used less and less frequently as the older generation passed on, as was the name of the other mostly African-American district, Stringtown.

Evangeline and her husband, John Soules, by then deceased, had ten children, one of them being Stephen's father, Danny. John had been an electrician and one of Scottsville's first black business owners.

The Soules are a close-knit family, and the children, now scattered to places like Indiana and California, come back a few times a year to reunite with their kin and attend the First Baptist Church, where Danny was in training to become a deacon. It is the only all-black church in town, an animated one-room building for the tight, family-like community. It seemed as if almost the entire congregation was in the choir.

The Soules had a long history of working for the wealthy Turners. Evangeline had worked for Luke's stepfather's parents, Laura Jo and Wayne Dugas. She was a nanny and helped raise Bruce Dugas. Danny's uncle worked for the Turner family for over fifty years, helping around the house and with the garden. John Soules often did work in the Dollar General stores. Danny was born on the same day and in the same hospital as Bruce's brother. They went to school together and were friendly.

Stephen went through his grandmother's den, passing the organ that Evangeline would play while she sang hymns. Once in the bedroom, Stephen took off his clothes. There was a feces stain on the front of his shirt. He strategically folded it to mask any marks and concealed it, along with his jeans, underneath the baby bed that Evangeline kept for visiting grandchildren. He then took a shower and returned to the kitchen to talk to his grandmother.

Evangeline always knew when something was wrong with Stephen.

"Are you all right?" she asked him.

"Yeah, I'm just tired. I need to lay down."

Evangeline's empathy for her grandson bordered upon a kind of instinctive, preternatural awareness. "She could sense when he was coming," says Stephen's father, Danny Soules. "She'd just get a certain feeling, and he'd come walking down the road. She could just sense him." Evangeline was devoted to all of her grandchildren, but Stephen was always special to her. Before she would formulate words she thought that Stephen already knew what she was going to say.

Stephen would joke around with her just like she was one of his buddies. He and his friends called her "OG," for "Original Gangster." He was closer to her than anyone, and Evangeline kept after him and his friends in a typical grandmotherly fashion, trying to get them to eat.

"You need some meat on your bones!" she would say, offering up some home-cooked delicacy.

Stephen was devoted to her, always checking on her, doing chores around the house, and helping in the garden.

Stephen went into his grandmother's bedroom and shut the door, since she was up and about and he couldn't sleep in his usual berth on the sofa. He turned the television on, got in bed, and fell into a hard dreamless slumber.

Stephen awoke hours later in the afternoon. On the television was an update on the fire at Poland Hall. He walked outside to the foundation with no house in the neighboring lot, took a handful of jewelry from his pocket, and dropped

it into the dark aperture of some cinderblocks and went
back inside.

He was using the bathroom and talking to Chris Bradshaw on the home phone line when the call-waiting beeped
in. The caller identified himself as Special Agent Richard
Vance from the Bureau of Alcohol, Tobacco, and Firearms
(ATF) and said that he was looking for Stephen Soules.

Stephen told Vance that he was "Stephen's cousin,"
and that Stephen was away working in Louisville. Stephen hurriedly ended the call, and then went to play basketball at the park with some friends.

The residential advisor who had been on desk duty told
Kentucky State Police detectives that she had seen Katie
come in alone at around 1:30 or 2 AM. She told them that
Katie hadn't signed in any guests and had taken the elevator.

The WKU police had each Pi Kappa Alpha member
fill out a questionnaire about the night's goings-on. The
Pike brothers held a meeting where it was decided that
they wouldn't talk about the fire around campus or with
the press.

The WKU police picked up Ryan "Possum" Payne
and his roommate. While Possum was interviewed by
Detective Kevin Pickett of the Kentucky State Police at
the WKU police headquarters on campus, his room was
searched.

Pickett learned that after dropping off Luke at the
bowling alley, Possum went to a friend's dorm room in
Bemis Lawrence and stayed up playing video games with
a group. This was later confirmed by multiple witnesses.
But Possum's description of taking Katie back to her
dorm was shaky.

"I got her in the truck," Possum told the detective,

". . . took her to Poland. And I was like, 'Can you make it up the steps?' And I said, 'Do you have a key to get in the door?' 'Cause I figured most doors are locked. And she's like, 'Yeah.' She said she was fine. Fine enough to walk up there. I said, 'Just go on and just go to bed and sleep it off' or whatever. And she said, 'All right.' So I watched, I watched her walk about—"

Pickett interrupted the recital. Payne hadn't mentioned the presence of Stephen Soules.

"Okay, okay. Let's back up a little bit. When you went to the Pike House, you borrowed whose vehicle?"

"Brian Moon's."

"And when you got out to the vehicle, who was in the vehicle?"

"Aaa . . . Stephen Soules," Possum hesitantly responded.

This would be the last interview Possum would have with the police; thereafter he'd have an attorney.

Possum and his roommate were taken to the hospital and agreed to submit to sexual perpetrator tests. Upon leaving, they met Brian Moon and Damian Secrest at the China One Buffet for dinner and regaled them with the misery of the rape kit: getting blood drawn and hairs plucked, and the questioning by the police.

"They were not happy about the whole thing," Moon recalled. "Ryan said Stephen wanted to go back to Poland to see Katie when he dropped him off at Bemis and maybe he had something to do with it. I had not seen Stephen all night after the party so I thought Stephen might have had something to do with it also."

Later that night, Luke was on his sofa watching the NBA play-offs when headlights shined through the partially drawn blinds. He peered out the window and saw Brittany's father, Ed Stinson, climb out of his van and head to the front door. Luke's stomach felt like it dropped to his feet. Ed, a large, grim man, was known for being very protective of his daughters, and Luke was already intimidated by him. Luke's dad had told him that Stinson had furiously called his house looking for him early in the morning after the altercation with Brittany.

Luke opened the door and Mr. Stinson looked even bigger than usual. Luke felt dwarfed. Ed's face was flushed red with fury. Ed considered himself to be cooled off compared to the night prior, when he had found out what had happened. With his eyes locked on Mr. Stinson's intent gaze, Luke took two steps backward.

"Stay away from my daughter," Mr. Stinson snarled and punched Luke in the face. Mr. Stinson spat some more harsh words at Luke and then turned around and left.

The encounter was brief and resounding, but not effective. The next evening Luke called Brittany and told her that if she pressed charges against him he would do the same to her father. Luke and Brittany both agreed to not legally pursue each other, and, shortly thereafter, were again a couple.

The next time Brittany was at Luke's apartment, the Bowling Green news was broadcasting a story about Katie's attack. Brittany commented on how awful it was. Luke was silent and shook his head.

CHAPTER 15

The days in the hospital were like a medicated dream, numb and never-ending. The lights were harsh and fluorescent, giving everything a sheen, an otherworldly glow. Footsteps echoed in the halls over hushed, whispered voices, as nurses in pastel scrubs scurried about whispering and carrying clipboards. The smells were chemical and clinical.

Katie loved pugs. Cuddling Katie as best as she could, given the apparatus that breathed for her, Lisa promised Katie aloud that she would get a little pug puppy. At one point Barbie, Lisa, and Virginia surrounded her on the bed and sang "My Girl." They reasoned that it comforted Katie to hear that song that she loved, that they all loved, too. They hoped it pierced through the gauze of the induced coma.

CHAPTER 16

On Wednesday, May 7, 2003, Sergeant David McCarty of the BGFD and Special Agent Richard Vance of the ATF went to Evangeline Soules's house to interview Stephen. Stephen told them that he had been so drunk he didn't remember any girl getting in the truck at all, and that he had never been to Poland Hall. He told them that Brian Richey picked him up from Bemis Lawrence and that they could ask him if they needed to.

McCarty and Vance met Richey at a Wendy's parking lot and he confirmed what Stephen had told them, that he picked Stephen up around 2:15 AM.

Despite her myriad injuries, Katie Autry held on for three days after the fire. On May 7, 2003, at 7:10 PM, she died.

Katie's autopsy report reads:

PATHOLOGIC DIAGNOSES
  I. Multiple traumatic injuries:
    A. Thermal injuries:
    1. 3rd degree burns to approximately 40% of the

total body surface area including extensive
injury to the genitals
B. Blunt force trauma to the head and neck:
1. Extensive contusions of the left side of the face
and head.
2. Multiple contusions of the neck muscles.
C. Multiple poorly defined sharp force marks on
the neck.
D. Associated conditions
1. Extensive diffuse alveolar damage of the lungs.
2. Severe pulmonary edema.
3. Visceral congestion.

Cause of death: Complications of thermal burns.
Contributory cause of death: Blunt and sharp force
trauma to the head and neck.
Manner of death: Homicide.
Circumstances of death: Assaulted and set on fire.

About 150 students were congregated in a candlelight vigil
around the bell tower at WKU praying for Katie's recu-
peration.

A Hugh Poland RA announced to the amassed sup-
porters, "This was intended as a support service, but it's
now a memorial service." The once hopeful crowd col-
lectively groaned and then broke into tears.

The specifics of Katie's attack would become more apparent. She had puncture wounds on her neck and bruising on her face. Antibacterial hand lotion had been put
inside her vagina, squirted in her purse, and also smeared
on the doorknob. The purple can of hairspray that had
been washed into the hall had been used as an acelerant.
She had been sprayed with it, specifically on her breast

and genital region, and then set on fire. The smoke alarm had been ripped from the ceiling and her afghan was tied around the sprinkler head like a makeshift tourniquet. The door to her room had been locked from the outside with her own key.

II

CHAPTER 1

Virtually silent since the fire, WKU President Gary Ransdell released a statement: "We will divide our emotions
between Katie's death and celebrating the essence of what
a college is about; that is graduating students and sending
them into the world to be successful."

Katie's murder could have been left to the jurisdiction
of the Kentucky State Police or the Bowling Green Police
Department, both of which assisted in the initial investigation. Besides the aforementioned agencies, there was
also participation from the FBI, the BGFD, and the ATF. In
a highly unusual precedent, Western's campus police took
control of the multifelony murder, rape, and arson investigation. This was the decision of WKU Police Chief Robert Deane.

"It happened on our turf," he said in a newspaper interview. "There was never a question as to whether we should
or shouldn't handle it."

Deane had worked on over three hundred murder cases,
but not since 1989. Born and raised in Detroit, Deane had
a long career with the Detroit police, working in the homicide division from 1973 to 1977, narcotics from 1977 to

1982, and then back to homicide until 1989. He then did specialized investigations until leaving Detroit in 1994 to become police chief of the University of Wisconsin–Parkside, a school with a student body of three thousand. In 2000 he was offered the job of chief of Western's police force and came to Bowling Green.

Deane put WKU Police Detective Mike Dowell in charge of the Autry case, the university's first homicide. Dowell graduated from WKU in 1989 with a degree in general studies (he started in 1977). In 1987 he was a dispatcher for the Kentucky State Police. He had that position for sixteen months before becoming a patrolman at Western (he applied but was turned down for other positions at other agencies). In 1995 he was promoted to patrol sergeant, and was in charge of the shift two days per week, a regular route whose duties included traffic infractions. In December 1996, Dowell became an investigator with the department. Neither he nor Western's only other detective, Jerry Phelps, had ever investigated a homicide, rape, or arson. Of the sexual assaults Dowell had investigated, none were rapes and none had made it to trial. He had handled two robberies (unarmed). The only violent crime he had ever been involved with was one of the robberies, when an assailant punched a taxi driver.

There was a knock at the door and Stephen's brother, Daniel, opened it to find Aaron Marr.

"'Sup, Boonie," he said to Daniel.

"He's back there fast asleep," said Daniel.

Aaron was Stephen's best friend. They were still tight, but they had been seeing less and less of each other. Their lives were diverging. Overnight it seemed Aaron had become an adult; he had a girlfriend, a job, and a daughter. He was getting his life together.

When they were teenagers, Stephen and Aaron sometimes would imagine what it would be like to have kids—of course they assumed that they'd have boys. Stephen joked that he would dress his son in a little suit and "raise him up like a real pimp." Stephen had always had an affinity for children, and there were always plenty of young relatives around. But Stephen and Aaron's main passion had been hip-hop.

For years, Aaron and Stephen made homemade raps together, and oftentimes Daniel would join in, too. Stephen's father, Danny, even tried his hand at rapping with the boys a couple of times. Aaron and Stephen would sometimes talk about what it would be like to move to Los Angeles. They called their amateur group the Wolfpack, and gave themselves aliases. Aaron was Fu-Marr, Stephen was Silkk, and Daniel was BS. Aaron and Stephen loved to smoke a few joints and drive around in the country rhyming into an old cassette recorder. Once they drove off the road into a ditch during a session and they left the sound of their minor crash in the song.

"We were like Butch Cassidy and Sundance Kid," Aaron says of his friendship with Stephen. "We were just the perfect combination. Our styles suited each other so well. He's a cutup, a class clown. When girls would pick on him he'd whine like, 'Quit, quit.' He was a flirt. Ladies would mess with him and try and pull his pants down, and he would be like 'Quit!' He was a wimp with women. He'd giggle. We could meet up on Friday night at six o'clock, everyone else already would have plans and they already have something to do, and me and him would be trying to figure out what to do, but I could go pick him up, we might have ten dollars between the two of us, but we'd come home with a girl on each arm and no telling what else, two, three bottles of liquor. We just was good like that.

We could hustle together. Me and Stephen always understood each other. Most people when they don't have black and white friends they take the racism stuff to heart. There was probably only a handful of black people in our school and I think most of them were friends with us, so, no big deal."

Aaron and Stephen passed an idyllic, directionless adolescence together. "Me and him done a lot of stuff together," Aaron recalls, "mostly drugs. Mostly pot, we did a little coke on occasion. We would have gone to the Bermuda Triangle if we knew there would be a party. Every time we went to Bowling Green was either to get alcohol or to party."

Once, they were at a house party when Stephen came up to Aaron and mumbled, "We have to go." Some of the girls had hidden their purses underneath the sink and Stephen had gone through them and taken the money.

"We went and got us a bunch of alcohol and had us a blast," Aaron says.

Aaron shook Stephen awake.

"Gimme a cigarette," Stephen muttered, his eyes half open, face puffy.

Aaron handed him one from his pack. Stephen lit it and laid back smoking. They both sat in silence for a moment, and then, remembering what he saw on the news earlier that day, Aaron jokingly asked, "Did you hear about that murder over at Western? Hey, man, I bet it was you!"

Aaron was just clowning with him. The pair would always make jokes at the other's expense and nothing was off-limits or sacred.

"No, it wasn't me," Stephen responded. "I was up there and I went to a party."

Stephen seemed so quiet, his tone serious. Aaron expected a funny riff as a reply, followed by a deluge of party details, whom he'd run into, the phone numbers he got, how wasted he was, but nothing came forth. It wasn't like Stephen. He must have just not been feeling well or was still half asleep.

CHAPTER 2

The morning after he met the police officers in the Wendy's parking lot, Brian Richey phoned them to recant his statement. He nervously said that he didn't want to talk on the phone and that it was best to meet in person. A rendezvous was arranged, and McCarty and ATF Special Agent Kurt Meuris met Richey at the fire station for a second interview.

Richey told them about how he had really seen Stephen at around 7 AM the morning of the fire, when he accidentally sat on him, that he didn't pick him up as stated before. Richey admitted that he was suspicious after Stephen asked him to lie, and he tried to find out what exactly happened.

"After I got interviewed with y'all," he explained to them, "common instinct, you'd go straight out and see what's really going on. So, I went up there to talk to him. I'm his own friend, and his story just kept on changing and changing to me."

Richey had found Stephen hanging out at a friend's house in Scottsville. Richey recalled to the investigators,

"He was going to tell me what was going on or me and him was fixing to fight. That's all there was to it. I done got interviewed by a federal agent and I ain't done nothin'. I told him to get in the damn car, so he got in.

Stephen denied having anything to do with the bike Brian Richey had found in his yard. He also insisted that he got to Richey's at 2 AM. But Richey knew this wasn't true since his girlfriend had stayed up packing until after three-thirty.

"I wanted to know exactly everything that he remembered," Richey said. "I called his brother after I done interviewing with you and he said the same story that Stephen told you all, that I had picked him up. I asked him why he'd lie to his own brother and he told me so his dad wouldn't find out and start nagging him and bitching and blow up about it. Then he turned around and told me a few minutes later that his dad was there when he got interviewed. So, why did he lie to his brother? I kept putting two and two together. He was lying—everything he told me. He changed his story two or three times with me and I'm his friend."

Detectives Pickett and David McCarty went to Evangeline Soules's small cottage, but she didn't know where her grandson was. Daniel and Danny arrived and Pickett explained their need to talk to Stephen.

That night at around 8:45, Danny phoned Pickett and told him that he couldn't locate Stephen. The officers returned to Evangeline's house to find him but to no avail.

Daniel tracked Stephen down to a cousin's house and they returned to their grandmother's. At almost 11 PM, Danny called Pickett at home and explained that Stephen was trying to eat and that he'd been crying. He told Pickett that Stephen admitted to him that he had been with Katie Autry and that the two of them had had sex, and that his son was scared.

Stephen got on the line and said, "My brother said you are cool and I can talk to you." Stephen admitted having sex with Katie but denied having anything to do with the fire. "If you let me get some rest I'll talk to you in the morning," he told the detective. Stephen agreed to get picked up the next day for questioning.

Pickett arrived at Danny's home the following morning, May 10, at approximately seven o'clock. Stephen and Daniel were still asleep. Pickett talked to Danny and his second wife, Valerie. Stephen woke up and agreed to get the clothes that he had worn the night of the fire. Stephen carried them in a green garbage bag and placed them in the trunk of the squad car.

Pickett took Stephen, along with his father and brother, to the Kentucky State Police outpost in Bowling Green. Stephen rode in the backseat with his dad. When they arrived, Stephen was escorted into an interrogation room. Pickett began by asking him to describe what happened on the night of Katie's murder.

Stephen looked like a gawky teenager. His nervously hunched posture (and extra-large khaki shorts and T-shirt) made him look smaller. His chair was backed against the corner. He had the aura of a skittish trapped animal, but his deep voice contrasted with his diminutive, boyish appearance.

Stephen told of his ride with Possum to take Katie to Poland Hall. He said that he and Katie had made out in the car during the brief trip, and that she had teasingly called him "Sick Boy." He said that Possum dropped her off, that he got out to make sure she got inside all right, that she invited him up to her room, and that he took the stairs because he was afraid of elevators. Stephen then said that he and Katie had sex, but then she felt ill and had to go to the bathroom, and that he left at about 2:30 or 3 AM and was at Brian Richey's by 3:30 AM. With some variations, Stephen repeated this chain of events three times or so, and admitted to speaking to Danica on the phone.

One by one, Pickett methodically snapped fingerprint cards down on the table like a fortune-teller laying out the tarot.

"Do you know whose they are?" he asked.

"Mine, I guess."

"So why would I find them on certain things I found them on?"

From the box he pulled out a plastic bag containing the purple can of hair spray that was found in the hallway and placed it on the table.

"I don't know. I was looking around her room. I looked at her fridge pictures and stuff like that. I picked it up, I was just looking around."

Their back-and-forth stepped up in pace.

"Somebody hurt that girl. How did things go so bad? What made it go so wrong? Are you covering for someone else, Stephen?"

"I didn't hurt that girl. Somebody kept calling the phone, I didn't know who it was. But it could have been her boyfriend or some shit like that. It was some . . . I was leaving, there was a dude standing out in the hallway. I don't know if he went in and done it or what, but I didn't hurt that girl. I'm sorry if that's hard for you to believe."

"So who was the other guy?"

"It was some dude—I don't know. I don't know who it was. I'd never seen him before. I don't know that many people from campus."

"What went bad in that room? Something went wrong.

Something angered somebody. Look, look, look. Don't be scared. I'm not gonna hurt you. Did the police ever talk to you like I'm talking to you now? They always yell and scream at you, don't they?"

Stephen interjected, "Is it all right if we just stop taping and go smoke a cigarette?"

"Do you wanna smoke one in here?" Pickett said, pulling out a pack of Marlboro Lights from his pocket and setting them on the table.

Stephen took one and asked for a lighter, and lit it. Pickett lit a cigarette for himself, too. Stephen grasped the cigarette with his thumb and forefinger, toked, and held in the smoke as if he were smoking a joint. He was hunched forward, deep in thought. He leaned back, exhaled, and said, "I don't know who went in there or whatever, but I did not hurt that girl."

"There's something that went wrong during the sex part, Stephen. Did she start hollering rape?"

"Rape? No, she wasn't hollering rape. I didn't hurt that girl. I'm not that type of person. I just didn't want to be caught for something I didn't do."

"Then who else went in there and done it? Was it one of your buddies who knew you were there? And you're thinkin', Oh, my God, I'm gonna get the blame for it? And one of your buddies come by, and you knew they were hurting her and you were scared? You didn't know what to do. You were scared to death. I'm getting pretty close, aren't I?"

Stephen was crouched over, his left elbow resting on his knee, his hand on top of his head. It was like a sitting fetal position. He nodded affirmatively in short, quick motions, all the while staring at the floor.

"You were the scaredest you've ever been, weren't you?"

Stephen didn't move. The fluorescent lights faintly hummed. He mumbled, "Scared to death."

Staring at the floor, but in a strong voice, Stephen said, "We was in there messing around or whatever, you know, we was having sex. A buddy of mine comes in there, Luke. I guess he knew the girl or some shit like that. I guess he had talked to her at the party. I don't know. He come in and see what we was doing, and he wanted to get some, too. He talked to her or whatever, stuff like that. But she wasn't down with it. And next thing I know, shit turns crazy. He just got forceful with her."

This was the first time anyone had implicated Luke Goodrum in the crime. However, the police were already familiar with his name and those of the other Scottsville boys who attended the party.

"Now we're on the same page," Pickett said appreciatively. "Look at me. We're going somewhere. You couldn't stand nobody to beat her, could you?"

"No."

"You just couldn't take that, could you? Tell me how crazy it got in there."

"Well, he got forceful with her and stuff—the sex, you know what I'm saying? 'Cause he seen me and he was drunk, and he was just like, 'I want some, too.' He started talking to her and asking if we could run the train on her and shit like that. She was like 'no,' she wasn't with it. So he starts being forceful with her and stuff. He started hitting her. Then she started screaming and shit like that. So he put a pillow over her face and started hitting and shit like that. So I walked out in the hall for a second and I just didn't know what to do, so I come back in the room, and they was in there doing it and shit like that."

"What if I told you that he already said you did it all?"

"I'd say he's lying."

"He said you got the hair spray. You sprayed it on her."

"I didn't spray no hair spray on her or nothing."

"Has Lucas been known to do that stuff before? Get violent like that?"

"That's why he was in Bowling Green. Him and his girl got in a fight. He hit her and stuff and thought the police was after him."

"He didn't tell you, 'You better help me or I'm gonna blame it on ya'?"

"No, I haven't talked to him."

"What I'm saying is, you sure he didn't tell you that night, 'You better help me do something with her, 'cause we're gonna go down'?"

"No. He was in there hitting her and shit, and I just fucking left."

"Did he say 'pull the pillow over her head'? Did he tie her shirt around her neck?"

"I wasn't really trying to look at it. It ain't nothin' you want to see. It just tore me up. I felt like I should have done something."

"Were you scared of Lucas?"

"Well, he's bigger than I am. You know, I'm not a fighter or nothing. But I was just shocked. I didn't know how to take it."

"Did you let Luke in?"

"Nah, he knocked and she got up and opened the door."

"Was he there when Danica called?"

"No, he arrived shortly after she called."

"You sure he was the last one up there?"

"Yes, because I left as soon as it happened, as soon as he was hitting her."

"But you said you watched it for a minute. Did he rape her, Stephen? You know what you saw."

"He was pulling his pants down and stuff like that. But I didn't actually see him rape her."

"Now tell me the honest-to-God truth. Were you there when he finished and started to set her on fire and you said, 'This is it. I'm out of here'?"

"No, I left and then he set the fire. I didn't see him setting the fire. I walked out in the hall and I stood for a minute. Then I walked back in, and I was like, 'I gotta get out of here.' "

"Which one of you put the towel over the sprinkler?"

"I didn't."

"Did he? How come?"

"I guess so they wouldn't put the fire out or whatever. I seen him in there and he threw the thing up like that," Stephen said, mimicking hurling something around the sprinkler head like a lasso.

"You saw a man put the towel on the sprinkler, therefore you knew what he was fixing to do. And then you really got scared. Didn't you? 'Cause you had never seen nothin' like that in your life. You're telling it all and you're doing the right thing. Lucas is going to come in here and you know what he's going to do, Stephen. 'Stephen did every bit of it. Stephen did it all. I didn't do it. Stephen did it.' Give me details of what happened, and I can shoot that down pretty quick. It was a horrible sight, wasn't it? Go ahead and tell me."

"He come in and started grabbing her and stuff, and she didn't want to have nothing to do with it. And she smacked him, and he started getting forceful with her. And started hitting her and stuff. I didn't know what to do. Ya know? Then he pushed her down on the bed and put the pillow over her head. Then he pulled down his pants and started having sex with her. She was screaming and kicking and stuff. I walked out of the room, stood in the hall for a second. Then I come back in, and he was still doing it and stuff. He just kept having sex with her, and I guess he got done and shit like that. I was just standing there."

"Go on. I know this is the hardest part. Go on. You're right there, buddy. Come on."

"Then he got up, and he was like, 'You didn't see nothing.' And I was like, 'No.' Because I didn't know what to say. I didn't want him to try to hurt me or nothin'. He got up, grabbed the hair spray and sprayed her with it. Grabbed the towel or whatever, something, and threw it up over the sprinkler, and I just left."

"Tell me how he did it."

"I see him spray the hair spray," Stephen said and mimed holding an aerosol can in his hand and moving it back and forth rapidly. "He sprayed it on the bed and on the sheets and stuff like that. He didn't say nothin'. I was just standing there shocked. He grabbed the towel and threw it up over the sprinkler. I was like, 'Man, you're fucking crazy.' He didn't say nothin'."

"Did you see him light the fire, Stephen?"

"No, 'cause when I got outside, I ran down the steps, and I ran. 'Cause when he started spraying the hair spray and stuff and threw it up over there, I knew he was gonna do something crazy, so I just left. I just ran and ran."

It was now 9:58 AM and Stephen's interrogation, which had gone on for over an hour and a half, was over. Stephen agreed to have a sexual perpetrator kit performed on him and the police began the process of getting a warrant for Luke's bodily fluids and to search his car.

Katie Autry, as a sophomore at Hancock County High School, 1999.

Courtesy of the Autry family

Katie Autry and Heather McMahon at cheerleading camp, summer 2000. *Courtesy of Heather McMahon*

Katie Autry at her senior prom, 2002.

Courtesy of the Autry family

Katie Autry and Danica Jackson in their dorm room, March 2003. *Photo by Heather McMahon*

Lucas Goodrum, six years old, playing with his stepfather, Bruce Dugas, in Des Allemands, Louisiana, 1987.

Courtesy of Donna Dugas

Lucas Goodrum in his Allen County High School football uniform, 2000.

Courtesy of Donna Dugas

The Pi Kappa Alpha fraternity house at Western Kentucky University, where Katie Autry first crossed paths with Stephen Soules and Lucas Goodrum. *Photo by Miriam Gross*

Hugh Poland Hall, Katie Autry's dormitory at Western Kentucky University.

Photo by Marcus Mam

Katie Autry and Danica Jackson's dorm room, May 5, 2003.

Courtesy of Bowling Green Police Department

Stephen Soules at his arraignment on May 13, 2003, at the Warren County Justice Center in Bowling Green, Kentucky.

Photo by Joe Imel/Daily News/AP Photo

Danica Jackson looks over a cell phone call log with defense attorney David Broderick, March 11, 2005, while testifying under cross-examination at the trial of Lucas Goodrum.

Photo by Robert Bruck/Messenger-Inquirer/AP Photo

Virginia White, Katie Autry's aunt, addresses the media after Lucas Goodrum's trial, March 21, 2005.

Photo by H. Wilson

Lucas Goodrum's mother, Donna Dugas, and his step-father, Bruce Dugas, after the verdict is read at Lucas's trial, March 21, 2005.

Photo by Robert Bruck/Messenger-Inquirer/AP Photo

Stephen Soules in his 2008 mug shot.

Courtesy of the Kentucky Department of Corrections

Lucas Goodrum and his mother, Donna Dugas, at the Double D ranch in Texas, February 2007.

Photo by Marcus Mam

The Autry family in the home of Virginia White, February 2007. *Left to right*: Barbie White; Virginia White; Katie's sister, Lisa Autry; her mother, Donnie Autry; and Johnni White.
Photo by Marcus Mam

Donnie Autry, embracing her daughter Lisa Autry, February 2007.

Photo by Marcus Mam

Katie Autry's grave in Rosine, Kentucky.

Photo by Kate Hammer

CHAPTER 3

Stephen's parents, Danny Soules and Jean Kinslow, dated when they were teenagers. Their on-again, off-again romance went on for five years before they married. Marrying a white woman caused a few raised eyebrows but no major problems. "We got our looks but we never had any trouble," Danny says. "I was a pretty big guy. We got our stares. She was a country girl; she comes from seven miles out."

It was hard for Jean and Danny to eke out a living and raise two children in Scottsville. They both worked a slew of jobs. The marriage suffered and they eventually split. Danny and his sons lived alone.

"The three bachelors," Danny says, "more like brothers, I guess you could say. Daniel worked and I would come in and make sure supper and everything was cooked."

The living arrangements were nontraditional; no one had a designated room in the house.

"Him and Boonie always cut up and carried on," Aaron Marr says. "His dad was always riding his ass about getting a job, going to school, not doing the irresponsible stuff that we did. He rode his ass about it daily. He had reasons, but we'd be there all day sitting and as soon as his dad came through the door, he would start in on him, seemed like that's all he ever said. I know he was trying to be a dad, but still. So they weren't real, real close, but close. They would only see the mom once in a while. Daniel was more traditional. Stephen was rebellious. Well, he would be a follower with people that were rebellious. He had the attitude where not all the time he thought about the repercussions."

While Stephen was taken to the Medical Center for the sexual perpetrator testing, Detective Pickett interviewed Danny and Daniel Soules separately.

Daniel said that Stephen had been upset since he had first gotten a phone call from authorities regarding the fire.

"I was just begging him to get this over with," Daniel told the detective, "to come here and talk to ya, that you're a nice guy. I could tell something was on his mind. I kept on and kept on begging him. I got so I was tearin' and all that."

"Do you know Lucas Goodrum?" Pickett asked Daniel.

"I grew up with him. Me and him used to be best friends when I was probably sixth, seventh grade."

Stephen's father told the detective how he felt about his son. "I just want to say I don't believe he would do nothin' like this. He's a good kid. He's been in trouble in the past for minor stuff, compared to this, but I would never think he would do nothin' like this. He's always been a good kid. He's great with the elderly, he's caring. I just don't understand how me knowing him for twenty years, all of a sudden just one day this happened. It's unexplainable. It's devastating. He's never shown any of these tendencies before. I yell at him sometimes, you know, cleaning up or when he was younger staying out two or three days at a time without calling me. We've had our worries. He's not talked back to me or anything. One time he hit the hood of my truck with his fist when he was mad at me. And I was real upset. We both let the situation get out of control, but other than that, that's it. I just don't understand this. I really don't."

With his next interrogation, held two hours later, after he returned from getting his blood drawn and hairs plucked, Stephen had built up his confidence. He spoke more clearly, and the general air of despair was gone. He described with vigor what he said had happened, and was no longer staring at the floor for long stretches not moving. There was a detachment to his retelling, as if he were describing a car wreck he had passed on the highway. Around his wrist was a white plastic ID bracelet from the hospital.

Stephen asked someone to fabricate an alibi, was the last known person with a murder victim, lied to authorities multiple times, and admitted to at least having watched a rape. Chief Deane of the WKU police declined to arrest him, and Stephen was free to go.

"I'm going to go get me something to eat," Stephen said. "I'm going to get me some food and I'm just going to sit at home and watch movies."

Pickett responded, "Appreciate it if you'd stay around and be where we can find you if we need you."

CHAPTER 4

Luke had spent the day riding dirt bikes with an eighteen-year-old buddy. At around 5 PM, Luke was driving the boy across the state line into Tennessee to buy him beer. On the way to the highway, Luke saw his ex-girlfriend, Zipper, and one of her friends outside of Minit Mart. He pulled into the parking lot and got out to talk to them. In one of his pockets, he had over $700. Like his father, Luke didn't trust banks (or cops or doctors, for that matter) and usually carried most of the money he had on his person. The rest of his cash from selling marijuana was hidden underneath the Styrofoam in the cardboard box his video game console came in. In his other pocket, like usual, he had his personal stash of weed that he told the girls about.

"Y'all wanna get high and have a threesome?" Zipper asked.

Before Luke could discern if this was a genuine offer, he saw two patrol cars driving toward the convenience store.

Luke shoved the plastic bag of pot at Zipper.

"Take this!" he hissed. "Put it up your ass or somethin'!"

The patrolmen took Luke to the Scottsville police station, where Detective Mike Dowell of the WKU police was waiting for him. Luke was driven to the Medical Center for a rape kit. Blood was drawn from his arm and thirty hairs were plucked from both his head and pubic area. He was then taken to the Kentucky State Police outpost and escorted to a small, windowless interrogation room.

Luke leaned against the naked white wall. The suntanned hue of his skin was heightened by his white T-shirt and matching backwards cap. He had long, skinny sideburns that went down to his jawline. On the underside of Luke's elbow on his right arm was a taped bandage from the blood test.

Officer Joe Harbaugh of the WKU police joined Luke for a few minutes.

"Joe Harbaugh, you the hardball?" Luke asked cheerfully after being introduced.

"Yeah, I'm the hardball, man."

The two discussed steroid use in baseball. The conversation then segued to high school football. Luke told him about how he accidentally fixed his bad knee by landing on it when he jumped from a bridge on a dare into the river.

"I swear, it was like a blessing from God! A baptism! My knee didn't hurt no more!"

Before Harbaugh left the interrogation room, Luke told him a story about how he once got chased by a donkey.

At 10:15 PM, Detective Pickett and his investigation commander, Lieutenant Eric Wolford, entered the interrogation room. Pickett exuded empathy and a gentle tranquillity. Wolford was gruff and mostly silent.

"I'm really curious why I'm here, you know," Luke said.

The officers explained to him that he was not being arrested and Luke signed a document waiving his Miranda rights.

"Basically, Lucas, we're concerned with last Saturday night, early Sunday morning up on Western's campus," Detective Pickett said.

"I heard about that," Luke replied.

"Start Saturday night and tell me from the time you was in Scottsville, go into detail and tell me what you did."

Luke told of going to meet Stephen Soules at the bowling alley and going back to Sarah Carwell's apartment and then on to the Pike party. Luke described the night in his usual manner, heavy on speed and free association. When Luke spoke, whole paragraphs came out in one breath. "Brian Moon and that Damian, that Damian boy. I'm not sure of that Damian boy. I think that's his name. I don't know this guy. I've known Brian since he was a freshman when I's a senior, you know. . . ."

Pickett asked him to get back on track and to slow down the barrage.

"When you got to the Pike House, did you notice anything strange or unusual or anything get out of hand?"

"I saw my friend, Ryan Payne. He left and dropped that girl. I heard she got burnt or something like that."

"What girl? Back up. You lost me there."

"They said that some girl, whatever, something happened to her. I don't know. This is gossip, so I don't know. Chris Bradshaw—he's the one telling me about it—that something happened to a girl over there. Ryan went and dropped her off. I know it didn't take him that long to drop the girl off and come pick me up."

"Did you see the girl?"

"She was in there dancing. She was really intoxicated.

She needed a ride home. She was in no shape to drive if that's the same girl."

"Was she dancing with you?"

"Naw, naw, she didn't never dance with me. She come by and rubbed on my stomach. She was dancing with Brian and Damian a lot. Everybody knew she'd been drinking a lot. There was some guys there that were all over her. There was a bunch of black guys dancing with her and stuff. She set outside and talked to a bunch of people. Finally, the police showed up and we left. She got a sober ride home."

"So where was Stephen?"

"That's what we don't know. Ryan was supposed to have dropped Stephen off at the dorm and he was supposed to be sitting there on the couch just waiting. Me and Possum rode around looking for him for a little while and we didn't see him. He's a friend of mine and I was worried. I thought he'd done got arrested or something."

"Have you talked to any of these guys since all this happened?"

"No, sir. I ain't talked to Stephen. I was gonna try to get hold of him, but he ain't got no cell phone and his brother's the only person that's got a phone. But that Chris guy told me about the incident with the girl. I asked him, 'Man, Stephen all right? He disappeared, did he get arrested?' He's like, 'Naw, naw, he's fine.' They said he had called somebody or something. He'd gotten a ride home somehow. And he told me what happened to that girl. I thought it was crazy. And he said they thought Ryan had did it. I don't think he'd ever do anything like that. He said they thought y'all picked him up or something."

"Do you think Possum would ever do anything like that?"

"No, sir. I graduated with him, played football with him. I'd vouch for him. I'd definitely say he wouldn't do anything like that."

The questioning led to where Luke had gone once he had left the bowling alley after Possum had dropped him off. Luke responded that he went to his father's house in Scottsville.

"He was up," Luke said. "It was close to three-thirty, four in the morning. We sit there for a little while and bullshitted. He's on my case, I'm not really a good dad to my son and that pisses him off. We had a long hard talk about that."

"Why ain't you a good dad? What makes him think that?"

"'Cause I'm a loser. I don't work. I worked, had a good job, and I quit like an idiot. I was trying to join the air force. I'm trying to do something with my life 'cause I never went to college or nothin'. I had an opportunity to play ball after high school. I didn't take up on that opportunity. I was whupped. Got a girl, got a baby."

"So you think women got a lot of power?" Pickett asked.

"My baby's mom, she was just so beautiful," Luke responded. "She had my baby. She had all kinds of power over me. She got pregnant before I graduated. That was it for me. I's in love. I's still in love with the girl. She's getting married and it kills me."

"Lucas, how do you feel about men and women fighting?" Pickett asked.

"Personally, I grew up seeing my dad do it. I was real little. I seen my stepdad and my mom fight. I've seen my dad fight with all his wives. I don't think it's right."

"You mean just fight them or are you talking like beat them down?"

"Naw, naw, not like beat them down. I took an ass wh-upping 'cause of a girl's dad before."

"You had a little problem last Saturday night before you left Scottsville. I know the answers before I ask the questions."

Luke reached up with both hands and shifted his cap. "We got in a fight, me and my girlfriend, Brittany Stinson. She left, whatever, I didn't want her to leave."

"Do you tend to get a little hotheaded?"

"Not anymore. I'm pretty calm. I've been to anger management. I did it six months. You sit and watch a video. It was court ordered. It really helped me out a lot. It calmed me down a lot. Most of the people that do that's bad white trash. When I was in high school I was hotheaded."

"But you grew up thinking it was just okay to hit a woman?"

"Naw, naw, naw, naw. My mom and stepdad they told me that's just not right. I know that ain't right. I don't open-face hit women or nothin'," Luke said and punched his palm with his closed fist. "I don't do stuff like that."

"Who makes you madder quicker? A woman or a man?"

"Probably the man. Guys can push my button a lot more. I try not to fight. I'm sure y'all know I've been in trouble before."

"It sounds like we are on the same page," Pickett said. "You seem like you're shooting straight from the hip. I'm a man of my word. I'll do what I say I'll do. And when I say I know the answers to these questions before I ask them, I already know the answers. I want you to tell me the truth. At any time that night did you go over to Poland?"

Luke leaned forward and quizzically asked, "To where?"

"Poland Hall."

"Poland Hall? I don't know where that's at. The only dormitory I went to was Brian's and Damian's."

Wolford, who had remained silent and ominous, like an active volcano, exhaled loudly. Luke turned and looked at him.

Wolford grumbled slowly, "When we started out this investigation, we talked to a lot of people at the dorm, a lot of people at the party. Put a lot of manpower into it. We've worked a lot of homicide cases, narrowed this thing down pretty quick. When we said we know all the answers before we ask, we *know* all the answers. It's just inevitable. I've worked murders before. People get a little bit scared. We can place the person/people who did it in Poland Hall by means of police video and by means of fingerprints."

Pickett retrieved a stack of videotapes from a cardboard carton and placed them on top of the table.

"Western has hallway cameras," Wolford said. "Not only can we place certain people in the dorms, we can place certain people in specific rooms. The death of this girl qualifies with forcible rape as a capital murder case. You know the difference between murder and capital murder?"

Luke shook his head and replied, "I'm sure it's both bad."

"Capital murder carries with it the death penalty."

The atmosphere plunged to grimness. Luke lifted his hat off and replaced it upon his head.

"I didn't do that to that girl! I swear to God!" Luke blurted, outstretching his hands.

"Who did it, then?" Pickett asked. He leaned forward and lightly tapped Luke on the knee with his fist, steadily, like a metronome, all the while looking him straight in the eyes. He gently continued, "Don't cover up for nobody because you know they ain't gonna cover up for you."

"Sir, I know that," Luke said, his body rigid at attention. "Brian and Damian was with me that whole night. And the girl saw me come in and sit down in the lobby of that dorm. I had on this hat. I had on a blue shirt. My dad saw me when I come home."

"I know you went to Southern Lanes to get your car. And I know where you went after, but you didn't go to Scottsville. Tell me how in the world did your fingerprints end up in that girl's room?"

"What?!" Luke yelped loudly. "Sir, I don't even know that girl. I don't know."

"Yes, you do know," Pickett said. His voice was calm, gentle, yet firm and insistent, as if he were chastising a child.

"Call my dad right now!" Luke said. "My dad will tell you I come home! My dad will tell you I slept there. My dad wouldn't lie to you."

Pickett glanced at the stack of videocassettes and queried, "How do you deny that you're on the tapes? That's what I don't understand. I can watch you go through the doors."

"I did not go in this girl's dormitory. I didn't. I swear to God. I didn't touch that girl. This is absurd."

"No, it ain't absurd," Pickett said. "I don't have to call your dad because I know where you was at. And I'm sure your dad is gonna say you was there, 'cause he's your dad. But I know different."

"I swear to God I went to Scottsville. You can ask my dad. Him and my stepmom both talked to me that night. My stepmom won't lie."

"But there's other people that says different."

"They're lying."

"Why would they lie? Why would people hate you so much? And not just one. Not just two. I'm talking a bunch, boy. We've interviewed close to two hundred people.

Every time I go through here," Pickett said, taking a large binder and flipping through the pages of reports, "I come up with Goodrum and Goodrum and Goodrum. Do you think that I come to Scottsville tonight and I did these tests and I looked at your car because I didn't know what I was talking about? Do you think a judge would sign a search warrant if I didn't know what I was talking about?"

"I did not do nothin' to this girl. I swear to God. Look me in the eye! I swear to God!"

"I am looking you in your eyes. And this girl's got a name. Her name's Katie."

"Well, I'm sorry about Katie. I didn't go anywhere near this girl."

"Tell him what Katie said at the hospital," Wolford suggested.

"Katie said that you and her were getting a little frisky at the party," Pickett said. "She told you what room to come to. I don't know why you won't tell me. That's the part I don't understand. I already know you went there. And I know who else went there."

"Because we've been told by that who else," said Wolford.

"I'm telling the God's honest truth," Luke pleaded.

There was a pause, and Pickett shook his head and asked, "Then why in the world would somebody else blame you?" He drew out this question and left a long gap between each word.

"This is crazy."

"Ain't nothin' crazy."

"I don't even know the girl," Luke said. "Possum left with the girl. He's the one that left with her. And I walked back with Brian and Damian to their dorm, set there and waited for a ride to go back to Southern Lanes, and I fucking went home."

"But you didn't go home," said Pickett. He removed some other items from the carton. "I've got hair samples from the bed."

"That's cool, bro," Luke said flippantly, shrugging.

"And when I get done, I'm gonna have a DNA sample. I'm givin' you the opportunity to tell the truth."

"Them tests will show you that I ain't done nothin'," Luke said.

"Then how in the world did your fingerprints get in her room?" Pickett motioned to the cards with black ink-marked smudges on them.

"Hell if I know."

Wolford left the room and Pickett repeated, "The tapes ain't lyin'."

"Well, let me see them tapes!" Luke sounded like he was in an argument over a pickup basketball game. "I ain't been on the tapes. I am one hundred percent confident. man. You can run them tests. It ain't me. Y'all got the wrong person."

"It's gonna be a long time before you see your little boy again," Pickett said gravely.

"Why's that?" Luke asked, his jaw stiff. Luke pointed at the stack of videotapes. "Y'all gotta run the tapes. You wanna do this thing? Y'all say I was there?"

"I got people that's gonna get up on the stand that's gonna testify that you participated in sexual intercourse with her and a lot of other things."

"Man, y'all gotta have some sperm or something like that."

"The only thing I have to have is people to testify that you were there. I don't have to have all that other stuff."

"Whatever," Luke says, his voice cracking like a teenage boy's. "Whatever."

"It ain't gonna be 'whatever' when it's jail time. You went over there and things got crazy. Didn't it?"

"I. Went. Home. I went to my dad's. I pulled up and talked to my dad and my stepmom. They were settin' there drilling me about being a bad parent."

"And you could pass a polygraph test just straight as an arrow?" Pickett countered.

"Yeah, I'm sure I can. Y'all run the test on me, man. I ain't done nothin'."

"And what if they come back . . ."

"That's bullshit."

"They ain't no bullshit. It ain't nothin' but scientific fact."

"I ain't worried about it coming back. 'Cause I know I didn't do nothin'. I can prove where I was at. My dad and my stepmom can prove that." Luke twisted his cap forward and cocked it to the side.

"You might be in denial. You might be blocking."

"I ain't in denial! I ain't in nothin'!"

"So, you're going to be settin' in jail for nothin'."

Luke looked at the fingerprints and said, "And I don't know how the hell you gonna get a fingerprint. That ain't mine! I don't even know Poland Hall."

"So, why are you getting so cranky?"

"'Cause this is crazy. You accusing me of something I ain't done."

"I'm not accusing you. Everybody else is."

There was an extended silence and Luke rested his head against the wall. They had been talking for forty-five minutes. Pickett stared into his own hand and nonchalantly examined his fingers. After a brief intermission, they began again. The back-and-forth covered much of the same territory and then the interrogation led to Stephen Soules.

"All I know is that Possum is the one in the truck with her. He's the one that took her I don't know where," Luke said.

"Who was with Possum?"

"I guess that Stephen boy. I don't know who was with him."

"You don't know Stephen very well?"

"Kind of all right."

"What kind of guy is he?"

"Off the wall I guess. I've known his brother all my life, grown up and went to school together. Stephen man, I don't know what happened to him that night."

"He's kind of crazy?"

"I mean he's just wild, he likes to party," Luke said. He let out a loud, groaning exhale and continued, "I don't know how y'all are pinpointing me. Don't you got more people to interview?"

"You're it!" exclaimed Pickett. "Everybody does a crime and they think they can cover their tracks. You always forget something. There is always just a little something left behind."

"I'm sure there is, man. I'm sure there is."

"Now, if you can set there and explain to me how someone can hate you so much just to say . . ."

"People are jealous of me!" Luke loudly cut him off. "I have a nice car! A pretty girlfriend! I don't know. My mom and stepdad are pretty rich."

Wolford came back into the room holding a file.

Luke, slumped over his knees, asked, "Can I go home?"

"Well, that's up to the Western Kentucky University Police. Western's officers are going to be the ones to make that call 'cause they're carrying the case. They just asked us to do the interview on you."

Luke wiped his sweaty forehead on the sleeve of his T-shirt. "Can I have something to drink? Y'all got a Sierra Mist, 7UP, Sprite? Somethin' of that nature?"

WKU Police Chief Robert Deane entered. The officers

excused themselves and Luke laid against the wall and shut his eyes.

At a quarter after midnight Luke was formally arrested, charged with capital murder, and taken to the Warren County Jail.

Luke called his mother in Texas. Donna Dugas immediately procured the services of David Broderick, the go-to defense lawyer in Bowling Green. Ironically, Broderick had represented Mike Goodrum in his divorce from her in 1981.

CHAPTER 5

Two memorial services were held for Katie, one for each of her families, for the two short halves of her eighteen-year-old life. Both services were open casket. One was held at the Pellville Baptist church where Katie had been a parishioner for the ten years she lived with the Inmans. The blood family's gathering was at a funeral parlor in Beaver Dam, near Katie's birthplace in Rosine.

Virginia was opposed to Katie's body being taken to the Pellville memorial service.

"Had I had my way," Virginia said, "she would not have went to Pellville. Katie had been through enough, She should not have had to go to them. They should have came to her."

The Pellville service, held May 11, went smoothly. The church was filled to capacity with over three hundred attendants. Folding chairs had to be added next to the pews. Along the back wall were uniformed workers from the Hancock County ambulance service and fire department in deference to Jim Inman, the EMS director.

WKU Police Chief Robert Deane announced to the mourners, "We are doing everything we can to bring this to a conclusion. And I want you to know we made one arrest late last night."

Deane didn't mention Luke Goodrum by name. Other high-ranking university staff, such as President Gary Ransdell and university attorney Deborah Wilkins, accompanied Deane. This would be one of the few displays of the university reaching out to family members.

The memorial service was stirring. A slide show of Katie was projected upon a screen. In all the photos Katie had that broad grin, a bright flare amid the melancholy of the occasion. The shifting photos were set to music—"Keep On Loving You" by REO Speedwagon, "Melissa" by the Allman Brothers, "It's So Hard to Say Goodbye" by Boyz II Men, and "My Girl" by the Temptations, the song Lisa, Virginia, and Barbie had sung to Katie at the hospital when she was still clinging to life.

"The investigation can serve to clear our minds, but only God's truth can heal our souls," pastor Chuck Fuller said.

"God performed a miracle," Fuller went on to say. "He has resurrected Katie to a heavenly life. Katie wasn't perfect; none of us is. Today she is perfect in Christ. She is at peace. She is at rest. She is living in perfect joy."

The ceremony closed with a beautiful speech by Lisa. She had been crying softly throughout the service but was composed and calm while she was speaking. Her head barely peeked over the podium. She read aloud a letter to Katie, telling her sister how much she loved her. It read in part, "She touched us deeper than anyone could have."

The Beaver Dam service wouldn't go as smoothly.

Danica was surprised to receive a call from Jim Inman and wasn't prepared for what he had to say.

"I want to forewarn you that the Autrys have talked to

me," he told her. "I don't have a problem with you being there whatsoever, and I don't understand it personally. But they have notified the sheriff that they don't want you at the funeral."

Danica and her mother went anyway. They arrived to loud murmuring and a fluster of movement. Barbie audibly hissed and Virginia's face flushed with rage.

Donna Jackson was escorting Danica up the aisle to view Katie's body when Danica stopped advancing. Danica was shivering and mired to the carpeted path—it was as if she were a jittery bride frozen mid-procession on the way to the altar. The mourners were as attentive to Danica's movements as if she were indeed striding up to be married.

"I can't do it. I can't go up there," Danica whispered to her mother.

Virginia, walking so fast she might as well have been running, intercepted them.

"We don't want you here," Virginia said in a loud, clipped voice.

"Why?" Donna asked.

"We don't want you here."

"Why? I don't understand."

"We don't want you here."

The women repeated this exchange practically verbatim; all the while Danica became more and more hysterical with grief.

Donna and Danica Jackson hurriedly left, and the flowers that they had added to the arrangements were promptly removed.

The next day's newspaper and local TV broadcast reported Danica's snubbing. "Why would her best friend get kicked out of her funeral?" everyone wanted to know. Theories ran rampant. Even worse, and despite a ban on photographers in the service, a photo of Katie lying in her coffin graced the cover of Bowling Green's *Daily News*. Her coffin was splayed in red and white flowers, the colors of Hancock County High. She was buried in her high school Hornets cheerleading uniform with a favorite stuffed animal.

CHAPTER 6

As her father drove, Heather McMahon watched Pellville slip away. The town hadn't changed at all since she'd left. Nor would it ever, it seemed. They had driven up from Florida to attend the funeral service. No matter what, Katie was her best friend. The trip there had been altogether silent, more funereal than the service itself with the warm embraces, speeches, and slide show of Katie flying through the air cheerleading and laughing and smiling, always smiling. When Katie first passed away, Heather cried and cried, and then nothing else came forth. She couldn't summon words, much less tears. Her body became an empty shell, a vessel incapable of anything.

At the church Heather had sat next to one of her high school cheerleading coaches, a breast cancer survivor. It was comforting to be next to her, this testament to life, and her feelings welled up and the tears flowed again and she cried throughout the service, her heart crisscrossed with confused layers of love and anguish.

Heather couldn't help but think of the last time she had seen Katie alive. It had been only a little over a month before when she had finally seen her, after two years of long-distance phone calls, emails, and letters. In March, for her spring break from a Florida community college, Heather McMahon had visited Katie at Western. Their time together started out so wonderfully, but things wound up falling apart.

Heather was coming down with a cold but nothing was going to stop her from seeing Katie. When her plane landed in Nashville, she felt even worse. Katie and Danica were two hours late to pick her up. Katie was at once so familiar and so different. Over the course of their separation, Katie and Heather had both turned into young women, and their growth wasn't in tandem, as it had been in high school, when their evolution was so slow and in such proximity it seemed nonexistent.

Heather rode in the backseat for the trip to Western from the airport. Katie reached back and grabbed her hand and held it for the one-hour journey.

That week in Bowling Green, Heather spent most of her time ill in Katie's bed, sleeping. WKU's spring break wasn't until the following week, so during the day Katie and Danica attended class and Katie worked at the smoothie shop. At night all three would go out to dinner and then return to the dorm and listen to music and talk. It was similar to Katie and Heather's existence in high school—nights spent together sequestered in one of their bedrooms and talking all night.

To Heather, Katie seemed to be doing well in her new life. She was working, going to all of her classes, and even hitting the gym regularly. She looked great, too. Katie had always seemed like such a "girlie-girl" to Heather. Katie would never leave the house without her makeup on or hair done. For anyone, especially guys, to see her with her glasses on instead of contacts would be a disaster.

Now Katie was even more concerned with her appearance, and would go through an intensive regimen even to pop out to the dining hall.

On occasion, the girls went out at night. Heather and Katie met some of their old friends from Hancock County at a backyard party. One night they drove around in a Jeep with an old classmate with the top down despite the chill in the air. They were laughing and their hair was blowing wildly in the wind. They ventured out to a couple of house and frat parties. Heather met a lot of Katie's friends, many of whom were black, which was a new phenomenon, but not shocking. There had simply not been many people of color in Pellville. And Heather wasn't surprised that Katie could be friends with anyone given her sunny disposition. But Heather sensed that the people Katie was hanging around with were an interim crowd, the myriad cast of characters a freshman finds before settling down with a permanent group. There were smart kids, jocks, and sorority girls, and everything in between. But this wide cross-section didn't seem a lasting formation. And Heather didn't get the feeling that there was anyone there to have as strong a bond with Katie as she had, to take care of her and watch her back, not even Danica.

Over the course of the week, Heather got sicker. (She later found out that she had a sinus infection and had to get on antibiotics.) A hurricane was predicted to hit Florida, and Heather's mom was worried about her flying home. So Katie and Danica offered to drive Heather to Florida. Then they could spend their spring break there.

Heather lived in Fort Walton Beach with her boyfriend and a roommate, who were both serving in the military and temporarily away on duty. Fort Walton Beach is a popular vacation destination, but it is known more as a family resort town. About an hour away, however, is a very different scene.

Panama City is a party town on the Gulf of Mexico and is popular with university students in the South. It is the first spring break hub you get to in northern Florida and is nicknamed "The Redneck Riviera." The bars feature body shots, beer funnels, and wet T-shirt contests. Later that spring, the owner of *Girls Gone Wild,* Joe Francis, would be arrested there for filming minors topless for his series.

The girls' plan was to spend the weekend partying in Panama City and then finish off the week in Fort Walton so Heather could attend class and work (the inverse of Heather's Bowling Green vacation). By chance, some of Heather's friends were going to be in Panama City. They had rented two hotel rooms and offered the girls a free place to stay.

Once in Panama City, they met up with Heather's friends at their hotel room. Heather's Florida friends had been planning on going to a club. After introducing everyone and hanging out for a bit, Heather excused herself to go to sleep. She was feeling terrible.

Katie and Danica didn't get along with the Florida girls. Even though it was her first time there, Danica vetoed all of their ideas for places to go. Danica and Katie felt that Heather had ditched them. Despite having a bed to split in the hotel room, Katie and Danica slept outside in Danica's car. Katie started crying.

The next day Heather had to go back to Fort Walton for school and work. Danica called some WKU friends and asked if she and Katie could crash on their hotel room floor in Panama City. Heather didn't understand why Katie and Danica had slept in the car when they had a bed. Danica was angry with Heather for not understanding why Katie was upset. There were hurt feelings all around.

The following day Danica and Katie showed up at Heather's apartment. Katie wanted to borrow two hundred dollars so they could stay in Panama City. Heather pulled Katie aside.

"Look, you're my best friend," she said to her. "Do you want the money to stay with Danica in Panama City or do you want to stay here with me? And instead of giving you the money now, I will give you the money to fly back home."

Katie opted for Panama City. Heather would have to see if she could borrow money from her parents. That night they all stayed in Heather's apartment. Heather and Danica's fledgling relationship had disintegrated. At best, they were civil to each other. They mainly just ignored each other while Katie ran interference with her sweetness.

The next morning the girls went to see Heather's father, Sean McMahon, for the loan. He was excited to see Katie for the first time in so long, but when they got there, he could tell that she had changed. This wasn't the Katie who was always giggling. Something wasn't right about her smile, he thought. McMahon pulled her aside to the kitchen.

"We used up all our money and we don't even have money to get home," Katie told him. She was looking at the floor and wouldn't meet his gaze when he handed her the two hundred dollars.

"I'll pay you back," Katie said sheepishly.

"You don't have to, you're like a daughter!" he assured her.

But Katie just seemed so unhappy to him, so unlike the Katie who had been Heather's best friend in high school and always at the house. He asked her if anything was wrong.

"No, everything is okay," she responded meekly.

Danica and Katie returned to Panama City to finish out their week. After Danica and Katie left, Heather shed her restraint and started crying.

It isn't surprising that the trip ended up being a disaster. It might have been subconscious, but Danica and Heather were both best friends of Katie, representing different times and places, and so in a sense were vying with each other. They were also very different young women, around whom Katie exhibited different behavior.

Katie and Danica ended up having a great time in Panama City. There were three rooms full of Western kids whom they knew. The two of them hung out alone at the beach during the day and partied at night.

Danica drove Katie from Florida to the Inmans' house in Pellville to finish out the vacation. Danica stayed the night. She found the household peculiarly silent, and felt that the Inmans barely spoke to her.

Lisa says, "In high school, Katie wasn't comfortable with her body. To be honest, she had a gorgeous body. She came back to Hancock County, and I won't forget. She's standing in front of a mirror, no clothes on, looking at herself. It was something in her eyes, a sparkle, and the smile on her face—she was grinning from ear to ear. At that point, I think Katie was finally satisfied with her body. In high school, Katie probably never got the guy she wanted, you know? 'Cause they all—she didn't have the right last name, I guess, and the money and the nice cars. But college, Katie was finally Katie. She could be who she wanted to be."

The souvenir that Katie had brought back from Florida was a tattoo of a butterfly on her lower back. It is impossible not to see a butterfly as the most obvious metaphor for change, and wonder if this is how Katie saw herself.

CHAPTER 7

On May 12, Pickett and Harbaugh went to the house foundation on the lot next to Evangeline Soules's residence. Stephen had told them that Luke had stashed Katie's jewelry there. The sun was at its peak. The cement was surrounded by a tangle of overgrown weeds and ivy. Pickett shined a flashlight inside the opening of the wall, and at the base, eight cinder blocks down, he saw a sparkle in the blackness.

The officers chipped away at the base of the wall with a pickax until they could see the jewelry clearly. They found gold necklaces and a silver chain wadded and knotted together, as well as Katie's class ring. A braided rope bracelet intertwined with plastic beads rounded out the hidden trove.

After being questioned, Stephen changed his story again. He admitted to the officers that, in fact, it was he who had hidden the items next to his grandmother's house, not Luke. Stephen was taken back to the station for more questioning. Stephen sat in an interrogation room and told Detective Pickett that Katie pecked him on his cheek during the ride, that he touched her breasts, and that they had kissed. Pickett asked him what kind of kisser she was.

Stephen laughed jovially and said, "About a six or a seven."

"When you went over there, did you have intentions of you and her hookin' up?" Pickett asked.

"I was just goin' up there to check on her. She was a nice girl, I could tell."

The desk attendant did not see Stephen Soules (or Luke Goodrum) enter the building. From 11 PM to 7 AM the doors to the hall were supposed to be locked and a key required to enter the building. Most often, the doors remained unlocked. Also, the back door, which was a fire exit, was used by the students to enter and exit the building, and was most often not alarmed.

Stephen advanced to the part where Katie changed into her bedclothes in the bathroom. He told Pickett that this was when he did his preliminary search and found the jewelry box, but that he didn't start "schemin'" and steal the contents until the second time she went to the bathroom to vomit. Pickett asked if he took money and Stephen said no, but that he had seen some in the WKU pouch connected to Katie's key chain. Katie's keys, including the one used to lock her door from the outside after her attack, would never be found.

Stephen told Pickett that shortly after Katie returned from the bathroom the second time, Luke knocked at the door of the room and Katie opened it and let him in. Stephen described Luke to Pickett thusly: "He does a lot of stuff that I don't approve of. Lot of drugs and shit. Shrooms, coke, Ecstasy, just anything."

Stephen repeated the story of Luke's attack on Katie in a calm and unbothered tone, occasionally illustrating by punching at the air. "And he starts tryin' to grab her ass and play with her pussy and shit like that," Stephen explained and then interrupted his retelling and excused his use of profanities. "I don't like talkin' like that."

With this interrogation, Stephen now said that Luke threatened him during the assault of Katie. He alleged that in the beginning of the attack Luke had said, "I'll hurt your family if you don't shut the fuck up."

"That's when he just pulled his pants down and put the condom on and just started fuckin' her," Stephen described. Stephen claimed to have watched Luke rape Katie for thirty to forty minutes.

"You didn't think that you should've went downstairs and yelled for help?" Pickett asked him.

"Yeah, but if I'd have done that, then he could've got up and stabbed me with something. I just didn't wanna get hurt and I didn't want my family to get hurt."

Stephen said that when Luke was finished with the rape, he thinks that Luke put the condom in his jeans pocket. According to Stephen, Luke then left the room to go to the bathroom to wash up and upon returning put hand sanitizer in Katie's vagina. Stephen claimed that Luke then forced him to rape Katie.

"He's like, 'Come here,' and I was like, 'What? Man, I ain't got nothin' to do with this shit.' And he says, 'You ain't usin' no protection, no nothin' like that.' And I said, 'No. That's gonna put that shit dead on me. It's gonna look like I done it,' and he's like, 'Well, yes you are. I know where your family lives. I know where you stay at. Something will happen. If I don't do it, if I get locked up, I got friends that will.' And after that, I just started thinkin' about my family and shit. He's like, 'Pull your pants down' and stuff. 'Do it,' and I just sit there for a minute and I thought about it and shit. And then he made me do it. So he makes me do that or whatever, makes me have sex with her. I pulled my shit down, put it in."

"What was Lucas doing?"

"He was holding the pillow over her head and he was choking her. I just kinda closed my eyes and just said, 'Let this shit get over with.' And then he was choking the shit out of her, man. You could see that her esophagus was, there wasn't much there 'cause he just had it squished and she was gasping for air and shit. I just tuned everything out. I said, 'Lord, just please let this stuff be over with. Hurry up and get me out of here.' Then that's when, you know, I get through having my erection or whatever."

"Did you have an orgasm?"

"Yes, sir."

"Where?"

"I don't know. I guess it was in her. 'Cause that's where he told me to, you know. 'Get off, or something's gonna happen.' I was like, 'What the fuck, Luke? Look at what you've done' and shit. And then he puts the pillow over her head and tries to suffocate her and she's like kickin' and shit like that and tryin' to get some air and he just grabs her throat and holds her there 'til she quits movin'. I don't know if she was dead then. She just quit movin'. And that's when he got the pencil down here off the desk and he poked her in the throat. He jabbed it twice in her throat and that's when she stopped movin'."

Stephen then said Luke put the pencil in the back pocket of his jeans.

"Why'd he say he was doing that for?"

"Said so he won't get caught."

Stephen continued, "He grabbed the hair spray down and I said, 'No. Fuck that, Luke. You done made me do too much. I'm already gonna go to jail for something that

I did not do.' He threatened to hurt my family again. 'Cause he knows me and knows how I feel about my family. Every time I go out of town or somethin', I'll go by and check on my grandma an' make sure she's all right and if she needs anything."

Pickett produced a stack of photos.

"Please don't show me no pictures of up there," Stephen pleaded.

Pickett flipped through them and selected a photo of the purple bottle of Aussie hair spray and handed it to him. Stephen studied it and gave it back.

"He made me, told me to spray her with it," Stephen said and mimicked covering Katie with the accelerant. "I just went like that. It comes out constantly while you hold down. Then I just backed up toward the door and was like, 'Luke, man, fuck this shit. Let's go. Let's just go. I ain't gonna say nothin' just as long as you don't hurt my family.' At that point he tied something around her, it was kinda like a curling iron or somethin' girls use for their hair."

"So he took the curling iron and did what with it?"

"Bashed her in the face with it," Stephen said, a cigarette dangling from his lip. "That's when it shattered. And he said, 'Hold this.' And when I grabbed it like that, I just dropped it. I was like, 'Man, my fingerprints is all over this room.' All I could think is 'I'm gonna go to jail for rape.' Somethin' I did not do. Somethin' I was forced to do. Then he just moved the pillow back and started lookin' at her and shit. I said, 'Man, I ain't gonna say nothin' as long as nothin' don't happen to my family.' The first time somethin' happens to my family I told him I would tell. He's like, 'I won't do nothin' to your family as long as you keep your mouth shut.' And I asked him, 'How could you do somethin' like that?' and he just didn't say nothin'."

Stephen then said Luke threw a blanket over Katie.

"Then he goes down to the far end of the room and picks up some paper and stuff like that. I was like, 'Luke, I promise I'm not gonna say nothin', just let me leave. Just don't bother my family.' That's when I left. I knew he was gonna light it."

"Did you see him light the paper?"

"No."

"Are you sure, Stephen?"

"Yes, sir."

"The other day you told me you saw him light the paper."

"No, I told you when I got to the bottom of the steps that I heard the fire alarm go off."

"No, you told me that you saw him light the paper and throw it and that's when you took off running. Listen to me. I know that was the worst part of it. Look at me. Hey. Hey. I know that was the worst part. But you saw him light that paper."

"Yeah."

"Look at me. Hey, have I not been here for you this whole thing?"

"I appreciate that. I just want to forget this stuff."

"We can't forget it 'til we tell the truth. Isn't that right?"

"Well, then he lights it and then he throws it on her and then that's when you could see it light up," Stephen quickly blurted. "And that's when I take off runnin' down the steps and when I got to the bottom of the steps and were goin' outside, that's when I heard the fire alarm go off."

"Was it like a big flash fire?"

"It just, 'Shewww!'" said Stephen, raising his right hand swiftly. He inhaled from the cigarette in his left hand and added, "It took the paper a while to burn."

"What'd he light it with?"

"A cigarette lighter."

"You know what color it was?"

"I didn't see it. I wasn't tryin' to look much at all."

"Did y'all leave together?"

"No. I was scared of him. I did not leave with him."

Stephen talked about racing to Brian Richey's house ("I felt like cryin' and stuff"), of stealing a purple "girlie bike" and riding there, and then sitting in Richey's truck before going onto the couch and the trip back to Scottsville. He then told the detective that Luke drove by his grandmother's the next day.

"He was like, 'Hey, you remember what I said?' And I was like, 'Yeah, just leave me the fuck alone. I'm not gonna say nothin'.' I told him, 'If you hurt my family, I didn't know what I was gonna do.'"

"Stephen, we've talked about this several times and you've changed your story a few times."

"Yeah, I'm sorry about that. The reason I was holding back information is 'cause I was still scared. My family, I didn't want nothin' to happen."

"Are you absolutely, beyond no doubt, tellin' me God's honest truth?"

"Yes, sir."

Following the interrogation, Stephen was arrested.

CHAPTER 8

Word of Luke's arrest had spread through Scottsville at lightning speed. People were shocked that the murder in Bowling Green could have been committed by one of their own. At Allen County High School, teachers left televisions on in the classrooms to watch for the latest updates. The school was incredulous when the TV news announced that Stephen Soules had been apprehended as the second culprit in the Western murder.

Amid the gasps and cries of "Oh my God!" one student quietly stood out. Stephen's cousin and good friend LaMont Preston silently got up from his desk and walked out of the classroom. The principals pulled Stephen's other cousins out of class and they were sent home.

"Everybody knows that was our cousin," LaMont's sister Kyeesha remembers. "You could feel people just staring at you and whispering. We left school for three days because they were afraid that somebody might say something to us to make us mad and we would fight."

Fearing the threats that Stephen alleged Luke had made (and also the constant calls from reporters), Stephen's grandmother, Evangeline, left her home and moved in with one of her daughters.

The Soules family knew that Stephen needed a lawyer. Danny called an attorney in Bowling Green who wanted twenty-five thousand dollars up front. This wasn't at all feasible. They then settled upon the more affordable Zach Kafoglis, a Bowling Green native with a local practice.

"They were good hardworking people," Kafoglis remembers. "His family talked about him being a good boy and he had never been in trouble before. He had pretty well cooperated with police the entire time. I felt he had a pretty good case, really. Stephen Soules is a victim in this case, too. He was a guest of Katie Autry in her room and had been with Katie that evening, was invited to the room, and it wasn't until later when there was a knock at the door that everything went awry. He knew the history of Lucas, he had known Luke from home and was scared and intimidated by Luke."

Kafoglis met with Stephen at the jail. "Stephen Soules was a meek, mild person," he remembers. "Strong in his faith. Was very close to his family."

In a preliminary hearing, bond was denied to Stephen and Luke due to the seriousness of the charges. Their case was sent to the grand jury. In the audience were Virginia, Barbie, and other family members, all wearing white T-shirts with a portrait of Katie screened on the front and "Justice For Katie" airbrushed on the back.

Eight days after Katie's attack, Western formed a much-publicized Campus Safety Task Force. The university announced that the dorms would receive new magnetic locks and alcohol would be banned from the fraternity houses. Once funding could be arranged, surveillance cameras were to be installed near dorm exits and entrances. Eighteen other recommendations were suggested, but not immediately implemented.

In an interview with Louisville's *Courier-Journal*, President Ransdell of WKU said, "I'm going to make a point this year, unlike in past years because I'm more conscious of it, of individual responsibility and prudence in your personal activities. Know when you're in a high-risk situation and remove yourself from it, and by all means be sober enough to do so."

CHAPTER 9

After petitioning the court, on May 28, Virginia White and Donnie Autry became coadministrators of Katie's estate. The reason, an Associated Press article quoted Virginia as saying, was that "Donnie is her mother and she loves her kids very much."

That September 18, Virginia and Donnie filed a personal injury lawsuit seeking an unspecified amount for medical expenses, loss of earning capacity, pain and suffering, funeral costs, punitive damages, and attorney's fees. Among the defendants were Western Kentucky University, the WKU Student Life Foundation (which owns and manages the dormitories), and Pi Kappa Alpha fraternity. Individuals named were the hall director, assistant hall director, and three Hugh Poland resident assistants.

In a September 19, 2003, article in the *Courier-Journal*, Virginia stated, "It's not at all about the money. It's about the whole world needs to know about this girl and Western needs to take responsibility and make sure it doesn't happen again." Furthermore, she stated that seeking damages was "probably the only way to get their attention."

The lawsuit further created a schism between Katie's

family and friends in Pellville and her natural family. Most of her Pellville acquaintances, including Heather McMahon, had never heard of this aunt before, and Virginia became more prominent in the news with each passing day.

CHAPTER 10

From the very beginning, Katie Autry's murder inspired a media blitz Bowling Green had never seen before. For years to come Katie would be mentioned in each new article about crime in Bowling Green or safety at Western. Katie's murder seemed to signify a new epoch. The crime became symbolic of the town shifting into its new identity, and all that can go wrong with a rapid evolution.

The heinousness of the crime and its savage misogyny would make it stand out anywhere. Katie's burning wasn't just an attempt to cover up evidence. The specific targets on her body were her genital and breast region; her killer burned in effigy what made her female. It was an abhorrent act, worse than anything the town had ever witnessed.

As the lead-up to a trial dragged on, Bowling Green also experienced the effects of the modern 24-hour news cycle. People came to expect the reports on every insignificant minutia of the case as regularly as the weather forecast. Katie's murder became a daily serial, tightly woven into the societal fabric. Virtually every day, Stephen and Luke graced the cover of the papers in their matching orange prison jumpsuits. The same high school portrait of Katie, smiling in front of a bright azure background, glared up from the newsprint.

But as Katie, Luke, and Stephen's images saturated the local news, the individuals became increasingly abstract and blurred. There was so much written about the three, but with so little information, that their story became folklore, altered each time it was retold and passed on. A familiar mythology grew around the murder, primarily reducing the key figures to stereotypes.

From the onset of their arrest, Luke and Stephen were pitted against each other as rich against poor. This came to the forefront September 17, 2003, when Western announced that they had accepted a $500,000 pledge from Cal Jr. and Margaret Turner, the aunt and uncle of Bruce Dugas. People were outraged and saw this as the Turner family attempting to buy the university off.

Luke became melded with the Dollar General store fortune, seemingly born into fabulous wealth and opportunity. There was hardly ever a news report concerning the case that didn't mention his Turner family connection. This constant bombardment of his supposedly pampered upbringing conjured images of him in virtual breeches with an ever-present wad of bills, which was quite far from his actual backstory. Luke was not close to the Turner family and did not consider them to be relatives.

Under strict orders from Broderick, Luke remained utterly silent. Again and again his stone-faced visage stared out from the television. He became a blank screen upon which one could project what they wanted him to be; and that was usually the incarnation of evil. He had an air of defiance, a cold stare. Stephen, on the other hand, somehow evoked empathy. He was repentant, meek, and also a victim.

Stephen was portrayed as the manipulated pawn, a

poor black boy taken advantage of by his rich white sociopath friend. People figured that his ethnicity had to have something to do with his involvement, that growing up mixed-race had somehow damaged him. According to his friends and family, however, this was not an issue for Stephen. It might have been for some of the fathers of girls he was interested in, but it wasn't something that he confided about to anyone, not even his other mixed-race friends. There was also a grudging form of respect for him—at least he had admitted playing a part in this tragedy, atoned, and implicated the instigator.

Katie became a pauper figure, an orphan, and a "foster child," the very classifications she cringed from in life. At first, Katie was known as the college coed who had been tragically attacked and violated. But once the papers starting reporting her tenure at Tattle Tails, the tenor of the reporting changed. Her murder became a morality tale, as if to say, "This is what can happen to young girls who stray." Articles never failed to mention her employment at the club. Although her job at Tattle Tails had nothing to do with the crime, it became a major facet of not only the way the media portrayed the crime itself, but how they summed up Katie's entire being.

A letter printed in *The Daily News* reads: "Autry knew what she was getting into when she applied for that job. She knew the types of people with whom she would be working. She put herself and her family in a position of potential danger and embarrassment."

Unfounded rumors of prostitution and drug use ran rampant, and the press mobbed the club. Rumors begat more innuendo, and a sordid hysteria about Katie's origins and the instigation of her murder spread.

This is where the definition of Katie began and ended for most following the story in the newspapers: the stripping foster child. As it was laid out, her untimely ending was inevitable, the sensible destination in a life of misfortune. She reaped a deserved and somehow asked-for fate with her rampant sexuality.

The family lives of Stephen, Luke, and Katie were dissected. Kentucky has the sixth highest divorce rate in the country, but that has not diminished the rigid, old-fashioned family values that are cherished, even if not always practiced. All three of them came from untraditional families, and none were local. Luke already having a failed marriage at the age of twenty drew some consternation, as did the mixed race of Stephen. Katie's mysterious background was simply baffling, and details for why she was placed in foster care were never released.

The murder and its never-ending coverage snapped Bowling Green back into a small town mindset. Bowling Green seemed to have been spiraling into a big city with unfamiliar neighbors, but now the locals who read about the case every day became linked through their scrutiny of these outsiders. Even the investigation, handled by the WKU police department instead of the state police or the FBI, became emblematic of the old-fashioned insularity that Bowling Green had nearly left behind.

CHAPTER 11

On May 20, Detectives Joe Harbaugh and Jerry Phelps interviewed Luke's ex-wife, LaDonna (whose new married name was Bowling). Phelps's report reads:

> Bowling was married to Goodrum and had just remarried on May 3, 2003. Bowling stated that Goodrum often used drugs but was not allowed to bring drugs into her house because of their child. She stated that he continued to use drugs outside the home and she could often tell what drug he was using at the time by the attitude he had when he came home. She advised that she was still in contact with Goodrum's family because of the child. Bowling stated that Goodrum did have a history of domestic violence.

"Luke is a choker," LaDonna told the officers. "Did that girl get choked?"

Luke first met LaDonna, a pretty blonde from nearby Franklin, Kentucky, at a New Year's Eve party.

"She was with this marine dude, Jeff," Luke remembers. "He liked LaDonna. Jeff was trying to fuck her. I guess she liked me more than Jeff, so he got pissed off about it. We got into a fight."

Romance bloomed and LaDonna and Luke became an item. For his senior spring break, Luke brought LaDonna to the Double D ranch in Texas with him. Donna Dugas made sure LaDonna stayed in the guest room. A few weeks later, Luke told his mother that LaDonna was pregnant.

The pattern of Donna's life was reverberating through her son. This was exactly what she didn't want for her children, and it had come to fruition with her eldest. She had cautioned Luke about this for as long as she could remember.

"I preached it for years!" she says. "Preached it! Preached it! Preached it! The last letter I wrote to him before I found out that she was pregnant I said, 'Remember, you've got football scholarships approaching you.' He made varsity his freshman year! I said, 'Keep that in mind if this is what you want to do. Protect yourself.' When they told me the day after graduation that she was pregnant, I had to leave the room. I saw the same exact repeat of what I'd already been through and that's exactly what happened."

Donna and Luke tried to deal with the situation, urging an abortion and offering to pay for it, but LaDonna wouldn't have the procedure.

"We offered to buy her a thirty-thousand-dollar brand-new car and a four-year education wherever she wants," Luke says.

On August 20, 2000, LaDonna filed a domestic violence petition against Luke. LaDonna wrote on the document: "We were having a fight on the way back from Bowling Green and he hit me, he also told me he wanted to snap my neck, and if he couldn't have me then no one else could."

Luke was barred from coming within three hundred feet of her. He couldn't own firearms or attempt to obtain them. He was also ordered to attend counseling. The couple was soon back together, though, and disregarded the court order.

Donna and LaDonna's relationship didn't start out on the best of terms and continued to sour when Luke and LaDonna moved to the Double D ranch in Texas. Luke attended one semester of community college at North Central Texas College, then dropped out. Luke and LaDonna's son, Tyler Goodrum, was born in December 2000.

Luke and LaDonna's coupling was never without strife. Their affair consumed them and thrived on negative emotions. Their breakup seemed imminent, and their friends and family weren't surprised when LaDonna left Luke and moved back to Kentucky to live with her parents. Many wondered why it took her so long. She took Tyler with her. Luke followed shortly after and they were soon reunited.

Despite the problems in their relationship that were obvious to everyone (including themselves), the couple decided to wed. Luke and LaDonna were bound in matrimony on June 22, 2001, in a courthouse ceremony in Springfield, Tennessee. The bride and groom were the only attendees.

"I took a bunch of Valiums," Luke says, "and we had a bunch of extra spare cash and she wanted to get married. And I was fucked up. I thought it was like if you break up you break up—you don't have to go through the court system. I didn't know what marriage was and she'd been talking about it since she'd been pregnant. So, I guess I thought I was stuck with her the rest of my life, 'cause of my kid with her or something. And I'd been partying the night before and I was still fucked up."

Mike Goodrum was ecstatic about the wedding. He

adored LaDonna and had developed a close bond with his grandson, a deep and reciprocated love that he had missed out on when Luke was growing up.

On December 4, 2001, LaDonna filed for a dissolution of their marriage and for temporary custody of Tyler. In a last-ditch effort at reconciliation, on April 24, 2002, La-Donna filed a motion to amend the domestic violence order. On it she wrote of Luke: "His conceling has helped him so much—he is a great Daddy and is paying for him [Tyler] on a regular bases! I want us to be able to be together!"

Their divorce was finalized that November, and La-Donna was awarded full custody. A restraining order was filed against Luke for terroristic threatening. Per court order, Luke could only see Tyler in his father's home with his father present, and he had to pay LaDonna fifty dollars a week for child support.

On July 22, the Commonwealth of Kentucky filed notice that it would pursue the death penalty against Luke and Stephen. Judge Tom Lewis denied Luke's bail. "I'm going to leave it at no bond," Judge Lewis said, "because of the nature of the case. I feel that's appropriate."

Stephen's representation would have to be taken over by the public defender's office. To handle a death penalty case in Kentucky, the attorney must have had prior experience with a death penalty case. Zach Kafoglis didn't have prior experience and he tried to get the public defender's office appointed to work with him. But Kentucky statutes prohibit a private and a court-appointed lawyer at the same time.

Public defenders Renae Tuck and George Sornberger were given Stephen's case. Tuck met with the Souleses and found them to be "a very nice family, cooperative, pleasant people. There was no dissension amongst themselves. They loved and supported Stephen."

On August 28, the DNA results of the vaginal swab from Katie came back. It was tested against the samples from Maurice Perkins, Lucas Goodrum, and Stephen Soules. Maurice and Luke were ruled out. It was a positive match for Soules.

Luke's lawyer, David Broderick, filed again for bail, citing lack of evidence, but was denied.

CHAPTER 12

It didn't take Luke long to realize what jail was like. It was locked doors, silence, and a stink so pungent it was material. A large black man was preaching aloud, his vestments an orange prison jumpsuit that matched Luke's. The television news was turned on and Luke's name was a repeated cacophony, his face a glowing portrait on every channel.

After about a week in the jail, Luke was moved to a maximum-security six-man cell for violent offenders. After his bond was denied, Luke knew that this wasn't going to be a short stint. He learned how to use the prison commissary and other basics from his cell mates. Some lessons he had to learn on his own. To get toilet paper, inmates had to knock on the door and a guard would bring it. When the guard got to the cell door the prisoner had to follow a circled line painted on the floor to pick up the roll. Luke once touched the line with his foot and got a punch in the stomach.

After a couple of weeks a large Mexican man was transferred in. After a few days of cohabitation, the newcomer decided he wanted Luke's bunk. This led to a fist-fight that Luke lost. Luke was still standing when guards broke it up, but barely. Luke was moved to another cell, and his brawl was reported on the news.

CHAPTER 13

Months went by, and Danica was allowed back into her room at Poland Hall to pick up her things. She went with her mother to see if there was anything salvageable.

Lisa and Virginia arrived at the same time, and went in first while Danica and her mother waited in the hall. The neon light hummed from the ceiling. The hall was filled with harsh artificial yellow light and spectral memories of Katie and Danica laughing and running down the corridor, coupled with hallucinatory imaginary glimpses of what happened to Katie on that night just beyond the door. It was as if Danica and her mother weren't even there, the moment was abstracted; they were on autopilot, going through the motions of this dismal errand, their bodies moving by instinct, their minds detached.

Virginia and Lisa emerged crying and clutching a few items. Danica and her mother went in. The room was destroyed, and what wasn't consumed by fire had been damaged by water. Police had removed the mattresses, and the bed frames lay naked like skeletal statuary. A half-charred teddy bear sat on the shelf above Katie's desk. The wall next to her bed was blackened with soot. A VHS tape was melted into the player. Scattered around was charred girlish ephemera: clothes, cosmetics, and stuffed animals—burnt—with vacant stares and frozen smiles. All of the clothes that had been in the closet had been dragged out by investigators and mixed in with the slop on the floor. Danica broke into a torrent of tears. This room where she had lived with Katie was now an alien landscape, foul smelling, completely strange yet familiar at the same time.

A few items had somehow remained intact in the wreckage. "How did this survive?" they asked, picking up different objects, such as Katie's cheerleading jacket or a cross that was propped against her bed frame. Some pages from a children's coloring book that Danica and Katie had filled in together were on the floor. Danica gingerly collected them. She would later get them laminated and put them on her refrigerator door, since most of her photos of Katie were lost in the fire.

CHAPTER 14

2004

In March, Stephen Soules was offered a deal for his testimony against Luke Goodrum. The Commonwealth would spare him the death penalty if he agreed to testify against Luke. In return, he would receive life without parole.

Stephen's father, Danny Soules, insists that they weren't given enough time to make this decision.

"The deal was something that got smacked in my face," Danny Soules says. He describes a phone call from Commonwealth's attorney Chris Cohron. "One Sunday morning I got a call, out of the blue. He said, 'It's either now or never.' Naturally that shocked us. It hit me like a ton of bricks. A decision had to be made then. Stephen did not want to make it. Because he felt that, 'Hey, this ain't all me. Why should I take the rap for everything?' It took me about three phone calls to get him to change his mind and he was not going to do it. I was looking at the death penalty, the long-term effect if this thing don't work. They're gonna kill you, and they're going to lethally inject you. That's what I was looking at, and I was thinking, 'I can't go through that.' I'd rather have him alive and in the penitentiary—at least I can go see him instead of go sit by his grave every day."

On March 23, 2004, Stephen Soules withdrew his not-guilty plea. He pleaded guilty at a morning hearing to the following counts: murder, rape first degree, rape first degree by complicity, sodomy first degree, sodomy first degree by complicity, arson first degree by complicity, and robbery first degree. The Commonwealth's Attorney's Office dropped murder by complicity and first-degree arson from the original nine-count indictment.

As per the deal, Soules would receive life without parole for the murder charge, twenty years for the robbery charge, and life imprisonment for the rest of the charges.

The plea bargain reads: "All counts running concurrent for a total effective sentence of imprisonment for life without the benefit of probation or parole. This recommendation is contingent on this defendant's complete and truthful testimony in the trial of Lucas Goodrum."

Wearing his orange prison jumpsuit, Stephen was sworn in. He stood next to his attorney, Renae Tuck. The special judge assigned to the case, Thomas Castlen, instructed Stephen to sign the plea forms if he felt so inclined. Tuck flipped through the stapled pages and pointed to where he was to initial.

"Are you pleading guilty because you are guilty?" Judge Castlen asked.

There was a long silence. Tuck turned to look at her client.

Stephen swallowed, then muttered, barely audibly, "Yes, sir."

"Intentionally, did you, in fact, on May 4, 2003, here in

Warren County, Kentucky, cause the death of Melissa K. Autry?"

There was another long pause. Stephen swallowed, and, even quieter, almost whispering, said, "Yes, sir."

Tuck gingerly patted him on the back.

"Mr. Soules, for the record, I want you to state what it is you did to accomplish these offenses."

"I was threatened by Mr. Lucas Goodrum so I participated in the murder and arson of Katie Autry and in the meantime I took some of her property."

The sentencing was postponed until after Luke's trial, which still had no firm date.

Following the hearing, Commonwealth's attorney Chris Cohron told reporters, "Mr. Soules has always given full and complete statements regarding the events of that night. We are confident he will give the same statements he always has. It's not an easy thing for a man to admit what he did in regard to such a horrific event."

"Mr. Soules did not ever change his story," Cohron also said. "He gave more information, and when the proverbial dam broke in his final story, it was consistent with his prior stories, but it was just a full and accurate account."

Despite her son's admittance of guilt (not to mention the physical and circumstantial evidence implicating him), Jean Soules continued to believe in Stephen's innocence.

"I know my son is not no murderer," she said to the *Courier-Journal*. "If he'd been the only one in the room with that girl, she would be alive today."

Stephen wrote the following letter to his childhood friend Derick Marr that was confiscated by prison authorities in a drug sweep:

4/16/04

*So how have you been doing? Me I'm hanging in
their. I want to thank you for writing me? Even
your cousin Aaron hasn't took the time to write
me. Yeah I'm doing OK taking it one day at a time
getting closer to the Lord. As long as the Lord
knows I didn't do those things to that girl that's all
that matters to me. His family is trying to buy his
way out and so far it seems to be working. They
payed my first lawyer off and the one I got now I
think they payed her off too. The District Attorney
came to me and said Life or go to trial and get the
death penalty. So my family was like go, take life
and leave it in the Lord's hands. I can understand
why they want me to do that before anymore
money get pasted around and I don't even have
that option. So I put all my trust in the Lord and
everything will be just fine. Thanks for the stamps,
but the guard just threw them away we can't have
stuff like that sent in. Be sure and tell your family I
said hello and thank them for their support. You
take care of yourself and thank you again for the
caring thought and support.*

Stephen Soules

CHAPTER 15

A year had now passed and Stephen and Luke were still in jail. But there was still no closure for anyone: Katie's real or foster families, her friends, or those of Stephen and Luke. There was loss and unknowingness and disconnection, all heightened by the deluge of updates on the case that really said nothing. Luke was awaiting a trial that never seemed to come, Stephen was in jail for an undetermined time, and Katie was gone. There was no justice.

On the anniversary of Katie's death, Danica, who had not lost her characteristic toughness, wrote a letter to the school newspaper admonishing the university for not marking the occasion. It reads: "Maybe you just didn't know her, but if you had you would no doubt feel the anger and pain that those of us who did do. I have to remember Katie and what happened to her every day of my life. I think the University could take at least one day to do the same."

Donna Dugas was doing as much as she could to clear her son's name. She hired a PR firm that drew up ads urging readers to visit lucasisinnocent.com. A letter about Luke was printed on the site next to a youthful, clean-cut image of him and signed by Donna and Bruce Dugas: "He has had his ups and downs in life, and, like all of us, has made some mistakes. But regardless of those mistakes, he is not a murderer. He was not present at the scene of this terrible crime and he in no way participated."

The site urged those with any information to write in or to phone a toll-free tip line. The site would be updated frequently with letters and video testimonials from the family. The family also organized a candlelight vigil for Luke in Scottsville.

Added to Luke's defense team were a jury consultant firm, two paralegals, and a team of renowned private investigators.

Judge Castlen placed a gag order to stop both sides from discussing the case.

Three inmates at the Warren County jail came forward with claims that Luke confirmed his participation in Katie's murder to them in separate instances.

The Double D ranch was appraised at $10 million. In a hearing on July 1, 2004, Luke's attorney, David Broderick, once again moved the court to allow Luke to post bond. Luke had been jailed since May 11, 2003. Donna Dugas offered a lien on the ranch, but Luke's bail was denied for the seventh time.

Lisa Autry was finishing the last month of her junior year at Hancock County High School when her sister was murdered. Her friends tried to talk to her but they didn't know what to say, nor did Lisa know how to respond.

"I didn't care about myself," she remembers. "I was like a rag doll. My body was there, but my mind wasn't. The only people I communicated with was family. Anybody else, they'd be talking to me and it would look like

I'm listening, but really my mind was someplace else. And in those last months of school, I didn't try, and I didn't care about anything."

In class Lisa mostly put her head down on her desk and slept. She was prone to cry; everything reminded her of Katie. It could be anything from a song to a cartoon. Her emotions were powerful, unpredictable.

When her senior year began, Lisa started talking again with her friends. But the relationships weren't what they used to be. The synapses had been cut, something was not right. "I think it was me," Lisa says. "I shut them out. I didn't know how to deal with it."

One day, Maurice Perkins received a phone call from Lisa.

"I just wanted to ask you, did you really like Katie?"

"Yeah, I liked Katie," Maurice responded.

"All right," Lisa said and then hung up on him.

Lisa had a track meet in Bowling Green and then went to spend the weekend in Morgantown at Aunt Virginia's for Barbie's birthday. By this time, Lisa and Katie's mother, Donnie, was living with her sister Virginia.

On Sunday, when it was time to return to Pellville, Lisa didn't want to go back. She decided to stay in Morgantown, although she only had clothes for a weekend. A few days later Lisa returned to Pellville to pick up her belongings. They had been neatly packed for her.

Lisa returned to Hancock County High to take her finals and to walk the line in graduation. The Inmans came to the ceremony but she wouldn't speak to them.

Lisa moved in with her mother to her government-subsidized apartment in a town almost as small as Rosine.

"It makes me feel like I'm twelve again," Lisa says. "All my friends used to tell me in elementary school how they would be cryin' with problems, they would go to Mom or Dad. When they would get scared. So now I find myself doing that, because we only got one bed. I'm crawling into bed with my mama. I may be twenty, but it makes me happy, because it was my dream when I was little to be with my mama. But now I am, and I wouldn't change it for anything."

In mid-November in Bowling Green, the holidays seem to be at war, clashing and colliding. Some last, lazy vestiges of Halloween and autumn are still out in full force on several lawns, contrasting with decorations put out by those so excited for Christmas that they can't wait until December.

Virginia White was at the downtown office of her lawyer, Ben Crocker, during this auspicious period in 2004. On the drive there, she had seen plastic skeletons dangling from trees, paper witches glaring from screen doors, and ears of colored Indian corn, haystacks, and other fall trappings stacked on porches. Houses directly adjacent were strewn with icicle lights hanging from the eaves and white wire reindeer paused in midstep on dead, leaf-covered lawns. As Virginia looked out of the car windows, blacks and oranges shifted abruptly to streams of red and green.

Virginia had on a pale lilac-and-green striped sweater, her dark blonde hair cut short. Her nose is slightly upturned, her eyes deep set and close.

"I have anger towards the college," Virginia said, "because it all could have been prevented. Katie could have been here today if they had locked the doors and the RAs had done their job. I believe they know I have anger towards them."

Virginia sat at a polished conference table, with Crocker silent across from her. Luke Goodrum was only about a five-minute walk away in the Warren County Jail.

"If Lucas Goodrum gets lethal injection, it will take away the worry of him ever doing it again," Virginia said. "If he is found not guilty, what do you think will happen? He got away with it once."

Virginia added, "I mean, I'm not a violent person. The only way I would hurt anybody is if they were hurtin' me. It's not my nature just to walk up to you and slap the fire outta you."

Virginia had been in a heightened emotional state, and talking about the case worsened her composure.

"For the longest time if you looked at me wrong," she said, "I would bust out bawling. I walked in to pay my insurance and the insurance lady said, 'Good morning, Virginia. How are you today?' And that was just it." As if illustrating her story, Virginia laid her head down and wept.

Virginia has her own theories about Luke. "I think Lucas Goodrum is a spoilt brat. I think he's always gotten his way. Mommy's always bailed him out and he thinks Mommy's going to bail him out this time, too. Maybe Mama and Daddy didn't really have time for him, shoved him off to a nanny or babysitter."

White believes Soules was telling the truth.

"I can't imagine why one person would say another person was with them and committed such a crime if they weren't there. Stephen Soules can't fix what he has done. He can't change what happened. All he can do is try to tell the truth to the best of his ability if it's in him, so that we can understand what's happened and maybe prevent it from happening again. I don't know what his creator will do. I don't know if he will get forgiveness for what he did.

He can't get forgiveness from me for what he did. To me it would seem like he would try to make right what he did wrong and he does show some remorse. My understanding from what I have listened to at the hearings and stuff is Lucas was an initiator and Stephen Soules was a follower."

CHAPTER 16

It wasn't hard for Scottsvillians to imagine Luke Goodrum committing an act of brutality, but the degree to which Katie suffered was difficult to attribute to one of their own. Was Katie's murder the culmination of a pattern of aggression? Luke's tumultuous relationship with his ex-wife, LaDonna, was well established, but his reputation for violence against women stretched back to high school.

All the teachers at Allen County High remembered Luke. With his hair sometimes dyed black or bleached white, Luke stood out among the other students when he arrived from Texas. Although he didn't look like the typical jock, Luke was a gifted football player. But most remembered Luke for his behavior and reputation rather than for his skills on the field. He was cocky and rebellious. The school newspaper, the *Advocate*, awarded him the mantle of "Teacher's Terror."

"He could cause some trouble with girls," says Steve Long, who was the head football coach. "He had a temper. Teachers would come to me and say, 'Could you do something with Lucas? He's causing problems with my class.' We heard rumors about girls and fights and possibly hitting girls and hitting cheerleaders."

Luke's high school romance with Aaron Marr's half sister, Ashley, was riddled with physical altercations and bullying. A pretty blonde freshman cheerleader when she dated Luke, Ashley later described a relationship that was precociously dysfunctional.

"He didn't want me talking to other guys," Ashley recalled, "and wanted me to quit cheerleading. We shared a locker and he took all my books and threw them into the trash. I had bought a new shirt that was kinda fitted. When he picked me up for school that morning he wanted me to change clothes and I said that I wasn't going to. And so he ripped my shirt in the driveway. He ripped it so bad I could never wear it again. He didn't want me to wear anything that curves my body and he wanted me to wear shirts that came lower than my butt."

On another occasion, a physical confrontation took place at school. "We had to write a fictional paper and I wrote about a trip to Florida," Ashley remembered. "There was a guy or something in my paper. Lucas would always go through my stuff and read it. When I come out of class he was at our locker and he started choking me and dragged me down the hallway and pulled some of my hair out." This led to a brawl between Aaron Marr and Luke, which Luke lost.

After Luke's arrest, his altercation with Brittany the night of Katie's murder made headlines, condemning him in the eyes of the reading public.

Luke was Warren County Jail's answer to Charles Manson. He was the most famous inmate housed there, and his notoriety grew with each passing day. There was rarely a day without an article or a segment on him and Stephen in the news. Luke got to know the newscasters. His least favorite was a reporter for a Bowling Green station who Luke thought always put a negative spin on everything, even when the DNA came back.

"If I could be in the ring for sixty seconds with that pretty-boy motherfucker with spiked hair to let out all my anger," Luke said. "Smart-aleck son of a bitch."

All of this attention made him a focal point for guards and other prisoners. Staff would come by the cell just to peer at Luke, to see him in real life.

Luke would be strip-searched before any court proceedings.

"You a little ho?" the guards asked him, laughing.

Days turned into weeks into months. Life was a gray expanse, never ending and never beginning. The only color was the prison jumpsuits, pulses of blinding orange floating through the static. The depression weighed so much it was as if he were in a pit, a dark cavern that deepened forever.

But Luke had to adapt. He read a book for the first time. And to his surprise, he actually enjoyed it. Soon a stack, mostly legal thrillers, formed near his bed, piled atop the sports magazines. Another new activity was playing cards with his cell mates. Some mornings they were allowed to play basketball for twenty minutes.

Luke's weight bloated. His thin face became round and doughy, his chiseled body soft and large.

The television was never off. A favorite show of the inmates was *General Hospital*. Luke learned the rule of *General Hospital:* "You turn off that, you gonna be hit in the face." Luke couldn't believe that criminals would be fighting over a soap opera, a woman's show. But then he discovered there were mafia story lines interwoven with

the romantic plots and he became just as engrossed as
they were.

"It's a badass show," Luke declared.

Visitation days were Wednesday and Saturday, and
Luke never went without a guest. It was mostly his family,
his mom and dad and their new spouses, and cousins,
grandparents, aunts, and uncles. Some of his ex-girlfriends
even came by. Most glaring to him though, were those
who didn't come to visit. His friends were all on the visitation list, and only five had showed up. It bothered Luke
most of all that LaDonna never came to see him.

A 2004 letter to Luke from his ex-wife, LaDonna:

*We have not really spoken in almost a year. There
is alot of things we need to talk about. Most important is Tyler. He is growing with leaps and Bounds.
He is extremly smart and loves to Drive. He loves
Tractors, fishing and playing outside. His favorite
movie is Thomas the train and Cat and the Hat.
Tyler eats like a horse his favorite food is Ramen
noodles and pancakes. His favorite colors are
Yellow and sometimes Blue. He has a Bird named
Blueberry and a cat named Socks, he loves animals
which is good because now I have a reason to get
all kinds. Doug says no hampsters or small rat
looking things. Doug is great with him so hope-
fully that will make you sleep easier, unless you
consider spoiling him mistreatment. I know that
you are in a Bind but we are too. Living expences
are outragous. I only make 6.50 and hour so we
are barely making it. Then there's easter, Birth-
days, and Christmas. Not to mention clothes,*

shoes, and undies. He growes every month or so. Your child support is almost 8,000.00 I know it's a lot but we need it. I don't want Donna and Bruce's money, but if that's all that you can do for now I understand. If you could pay me as you can, it is greatly needed.

Now on to visitation, I know that you've been wanting to see him (or that's what Mike says) but Jail is really hard to understand for a three year old. He has no physical contact which is something he needs. He doesn't understand why he can only get to talk to you on the phone. Last time he didn't ask questions, but it don't mean that he will not.

Lucas, I want too ask you If you have a Bible or can get one. If you don't I'll send you one, I want you to know that all of my family prays that you get saved. Jesus Is the only thing that will help you keep your head held High. I know you hearing me say this is a far cry from the person you remember, but the person you remember has turned her life around. When all this happened I about lost my mind. I was so confused, hurt and let down. I rolled in all my pain and sorrow for a good three months until I picked up my Bible and started reading. I gave Tyler to the Lord and gave myself to him also. I know your thinking why is she saying all this Its stupid; But caring and understanding comes through an open heart. Love and forgiveness comes through the word and my heart is filled with all. Your heart could care and love, understand and forgive once you open it.

Just remember your in our thoughts and prayers.

CHAPTER 1

2005

Kentucky lies in the middle of America, but its natives don't acknowledge its midlevel locale. It is a truly Southern state in mind-set, if not in exact physical location, resulting in a singularly dichotomous existence. Kentuckians consider themselves Southerners through and through and are also deemed so by their brethren below the Mason-Dixon Line. Florida might be geographically below Kentucky, but it isn't *Southern* like Kentucky is.

Kentucky's varied landscape is a rough-hewn mixture of brown fields of tobacco and coal mines contrasting with tracts of its famous flora, bluegrass, in the counties surrounding Lexington. There are tiny ramshackle mountain towns and regal cities such as Louisville. The accent is rougher, less lilting, harder than the gentler drawl of Georgia or Alabama.

While the geographic placement of Bowling Green between Louisville and Nashville was strategic for economic growth, it also made it a tactical site in the Civil War. Kentucky was a land of contradictions in the War

Between the States. It was the birthplace to the presidents of both factions, Abraham Lincoln and Jefferson Davis. Failing an attempt to remain neutral, Kentucky became both a Union and a Confederate member, divided between the North and the South. The Confederate capital of Kentucky, albeit short-lived, was Bowling Green.

Like the state that held them and that they were born in, Katie, Luke, and Stephen belonged everywhere and nowhere. Each of them was a nexus, divided between families, class, race, and wealth. Luke was rich and poor. Katie had two families and no home of her own. Stephen hovered between black and white. As fate would have it, their names were now linked forever.

As spring approached, Lucas Goodrum's trial drew near. It was scheduled for March and was moved sixty miles to Owensboro due to the pretrial publicity that had blanketed Bowling Green since May 2003. A telephone survey submitted by the defense showed that 97 percent of those questioned in Bowling Green were familiar with the case.

Owensboro is the third-largest city in Kentucky. (Bowling Green is the fourth.) Although Owensboro has more people, it seems smaller than Bowling Green. Owensboro is more rural and is dependent on agriculture. The farms in the surrounding counties send their product here to be put on barges to be shipped on the Ohio River. Owensboro has a lot of colleges, but none as large and influential as Western. Owensboro has a large Catholic population and more of a Democratic slant than Bowling Green. The town is also well-known for its barbecue offerings and a specialty, burgoo, a lamb stew.

Another claim to fame for Owensboro is that it was the site of the last public hanging in the United States, on August 14, 1936. The execution of Rainey Bethea was much more than a legal matter or even eye-for-eye retribution: it was entertainment, a chance for friends and family to come together and picnic and watch a man die.

On June 7, 1936, a seventy-year-old white woman named Lischia Edwards was raped and strangled during a burglary at her house. Using a new crime-fighting technique, fingerprinting, the police implicated Bethea, a black man with an extensive criminal record, who had previously been incarcerated for nonviolent thefts. Bethea confessed to the crime. He was only charged with rape, however, and not murder. The reason was that under Kentucky law additional charges of murder and robbery would have merited a death by electrocution at the state penitentiary in Eddyville, thus delaying his execution.

Bethea's crime garnered worldwide attention when it was revealed that the hangman was supposed to be a woman—she had inherited the post of sheriff after her husband died. An estimated crowd of twenty thousand came to witness the female executioner. Hotels were filled to capacity. Many locals had pre-hanging house parties. Newspapers from all the major U.S. cities sent reporters to Owensboro to cover the spectacle.

A male deputy ended up unleashing the trapdoor, much to the reporters' chagrin. Without the key gimmick of a female executioner, the papers pushed an angle that Owensboro was the epicenter of a death bacchanalia. The headline of the *Philadelphia Record* read "They Ate Hot Dogs While Man Died On The Gallows."

The lurid, sensationalistic publicity was an embarrassment to Kentucky, and public executions were thereafter outlawed.

CHAPTER 2

The long-awaited trial, *Commonwealth of Kentucky v. Lucas Bryan Goodrum* began on March 9, 2005. Commonwealth's attorney Chris Cohron represented the people of Kentucky. David Broderick defended Luke Goodrum.

Broderick is a balding peacock of a man who wears gold-rimmed wire eyeglasses that accentuate his penetrating stare and a different three-piece suit every day. His regalia is just flashy enough to exude opulence without going overboard. In court, Broderick is a natural showman. He proudly and deftly paces in front of the jury, projecting both his voice and confidence.

Broderick might have been the most well-known attorney in Bowling Green, but that didn't mean he was the most liked.

"David would defend Hitler if given a chance," was how one local described him. Another said, "Well, if I ever killed somebody I sure as hell would get Broderick as my lawyer."

Broderick had the reputation of being arrogant and aggressive. No matter if you liked him or not, you knew that he was good at what he did. The courtroom was his natural habitat, and confidence was his strength.

Broderick personally likened his circumstance to that of Rhodes K. Myers, a well-known defense attorney and former lieutenant governor of Kentucky.

"He was a phenomenal trial lawyer," Broderick would later say. "An old World World War II hero named General Denhart was accused of murdering and raping a girl in Henry County. Rhodes defended him. The first trial was a hung jury and then they moved it to Shelby County. The first day of trial after jury selection General Denhart and Rhodes K. Myers came out and the girl's brother assassinated Denhart in the street in Shelbyville."

When the gun was pointed at Myers, he responded, "Don't shoot me, I'm just the lawyer." This adage can be read to this day on signs in many Kentucky law offices.

"I always think about that," Broderick continues. "I really enjoy what I do."

During the trial, Luke sat at a table surrounded by the rest of the defense team: Broderick's associate Kevin Hackworth and two paralegals equipped with laptop computers with various prepared PowerPoint demonstrations. Wearing a sport coat that was too large, Luke appeared boyish, as if he wasn't used to wearing dress-up clothes. He was clean-shaven with well-kempt hair. But despite his boyish trappings, the aura that people in the courtroom said he gave off was that of a notorious murderer, his innocent appearance perverse.

At the prosecution table sat Cohron, Assistant Commonwealth Attorney Mike Pearson, and WKU police detective Mike Dowell, a ruddy, red-faced man with close-set eyes and darkening strawberry-blond hair. Dowell was prone to frowning throughout the proceedings. Pearson gave off an even more severe air. He was in his late fifties but seemed older. His hair was fully gray, and he seemed pewter from head to toe. He had the air of a retired drill sergeant. Pearson's voice was gruff and his brow permanently wrinkled into a sour expression.

Cohron shifted back and forth on his feet. He was a massive man, a former all-state defensive tackle for Bowling Green High School. Cohron had attended Vanderbilt on a full scholarship for football, but lacked the footwork to play in the Southeastern Conference. He had a youthful, red-tinged face and was wearing an ill-fitting rhinogray suit. He spoke in a breathy, jowly voice that emanated from the roof of his mouth, mostly in monotone. Whereas Broderick exuded theatricality, Cohron was more subdued.

Moving the trial to Owensboro was beneficial. The courtroom was crowded but not overwhelmed with spectators, as it surely would have been in Bowling Green. Judge Thomas Castlen presided with a restrained, even temper and gentle humor. He had a large bag of cough drops and would offer them to the jury and spectators. Castlen was prone to using droll, folksy phrases when speaking to the lawyers when the jury wasn't present. "Hell's bells, David," he exasperatedly said to Broderick, who was always eager to offer up an objection.

The gallery was split down the middle, reminiscent of a bizarre, ill-matched wedding. The right half consisted of the Goodrum-Dugas relatives, a phalanx in sedate black. Donna was always dressed demurely, her jewelry simple yet large and prominent, her hair short and frosted. Her only physical resemblance to Luke was their constant gum chewing—sometimes it synchronized. Bruce Dugas had a Caesar haircut and with his typical multicolored sweater underneath a blazer looked like a visiting Italian businessman. The family's press agent, a young, pretty, unobtrusive woman who could have been a cousin, always flanked Donna. Scattered anonymously among the spectators were members of the PR firm and assorted private investigators. The family and the defense team were staying just a few blocks away from the Justice Center at the Executive Inn, whose management kept a limo parked outside the front entrance to remind passersby of its luxury.

The left half was Katie's relatives. The Inmans sat somberly together near the back row, away from the Autrys. Katie's blood kin occupied the second row, right behind the members of the press. All of the Kentucky papers of any significance and TV stations had reporters at the trial. Also filing daily dispatches were the WKU school paper, the wire services, and public radio. Virginia White was at every session, and gave interviews at the closing of each day's proceedings. By this point she knew most of the reporters personally, and would phone them after the day's session to point out any nuances that she had observed and thought they might have missed.

Virginia usually drove the forty-five minutes each day from Morgantown by herself. Occasionally one of her brothers would accompany her, but all in all, the Autry side was comprised of only female family members. The women—sisters-in-law, aunts, and cousins—usually came dressed casually, many wearing candy-colored pastel sweaters and sweatshirts that contrasted with their grief-stricken faces, as well as with the dark attire of the opposing side.

While the lawyers battled with witnesses on the stand, the families subtly fought with loaded glances. During the wait to enter the building through the metal detector, or inside at the elevator, during recesses, tension between the two clans was unbearable. Everyone tried their hardest not to look the other in the eye. There were also the Souleses to contend with, many of whom had been subpoenaed as witnesses but who wouldn't end up being called to the stand. They waited out in the hallway.

No physical evidence was ever found to link Luke Goodrum to Katie Autry or room 214. The DNA found in Katie's body belonged to Stephen Soules. The fingerprints Detective Pickett displayed during the interview with Luke were actually the detective's own. Contrary to the detective's remarks in interrogation, videos of Luke in Hugh Poland Hall did not exist; the university had not installed cameras in the dorm.

Luke's former roommate, Matt Hire, gave some of the most persuasive testimony regarding Luke's behavior. He said that Luke returned to their apartment the day of the murder at approximately 5–6 AM and that Luke slept in his closet for about three nights afterward.

Danica Jackson, sad and affecting in a cowl-necked sweater, testified to thinking she heard two male voices during the final phone call to Katie when she spoke to Stephen Soules.

The three men who were intended to be the prosecution's star witnesses against Luke had crossed paths with him at different points in his jail experience. Prison snitches are not the most desirable or reliable witnesses, but the Commonwealth appeared to have had no choice but to call them. After each testimony, it became apparent that having no witnesses might have been better than using these three gentlemen.

First up was Terry Campbell, a self-described "outlaw," who had been incarcerated with Luke for two days in May 2003. Campbell had the air of a demented Santa

Claus with his full white beard and greasy, slicked-back brown hair. He hunched over the microphone in a sweatshirt. In a gnarled rasp, Campbell claimed that Luke had talked to him about the case and Katie. He went on to repeat details to the case that were a matter of public record. Upon cross-examination it was revealed that after coming forward with information about Luke, Campbell, who was being held in lieu of $100,000 bond, was freed without having to post bail and was simply signed out by his girlfriend. Shortly after gaining freedom, Campbell's girlfriend had some trouble with the law and an outstanding warrant. She escaped arrest after Campbell threatened not to testify. Campbell also had a run-in with WKU police and told them to call Detective Dowell or he wouldn't testify against Luke.

The next ex-inmate on the stand was Richard Mealer. Mealer, aka Little Redneck, Gator, and Wolfman, blinked his eyes firmly and rapidly and swiveled animatedly in his chair in his plaid sweater of all the colors in the rainbow.

When asked by Cohron how he brought information on Luke to the authorities' attention, Mealer calmly answered, "I wound up going to the jail because of my younger sister. I was put in there because I was living at my home on State Street before all this incident had happened. She come over to my house, tried to get up an argument started. And she had got caught throwing lies at my house, and she did not like that. She pulls a knife on me and I wind up going to jail just for self-defending my own. I wind up having a one-year probation, a six months of domestic violence counseling class, not including a three-year EPO [emergency protective order] between each other."

"Well, now what was the question?" Judge Castlen asked.

Cohron quickly passed Mealer on to the defense.

Broderick started out with "Have you ever told a judge or written a letter to anybody saying that you were a compulsive liar?"

"No, I have not. I have written a letter to a judge about my sister being a compulsive liar."

Broderick instructed Mealer to read from a letter he had written to a judge.

"I am a compulsive liar and a thief and I'm sorry for what I've done," Mealer said.

Mealer defended himself saying, "I'm thirty-one years old now. I'm grown up. I'm a preacher within a church that I go to."

Later, during the cross-examination, Broderick was able to establish that Mealer had fetal alcohol syndrome, ADHD, and was certified to be mentally retarded.

"The ADHD and fetal alcohol syndrome is really not bothering me none," Mealer said, adding, "I can't keep nothin' in my head because I have what's called a loss of memories, too."

The prosecution rounded out this troika with Micah West, a nervous, skinny, fast-talking twenty-six-year-old. West was in the same cell block as Luke for forty-five minutes when Luke was first brought in on May 10, 2003, after the lengthy interrogation with Detective Pickett. West had been arrested for using a stolen check to shop at Walmart. After agreeing to testify against Luke, West's pending felony charges of forgery and theft by unlawful taking of over $300 were amended to misdemeanors and he was freed on probation.

West testified that Luke admitted the crime to him while they split a bunk.

"And from what I could tell," West said, "he didn't feel bad about it at all."

When asked by the defense why the other ten to fifteen

people around them didn't hear this conversation, West answered, "Maybe he wasn't talking that loud. I'm not for sure."

Luke had been held in jail since May 2003 on the word of Stephen Soules and these three inmates.

CHAPTER 3

The courtroom drew a collective breath when Stephen Soules was announced as the next witness. Guards brought him to the stand from a holding cell, intensifying the sense of performance and the courtroom drama with a drawn-out arrival. Stephen finally emerged wearing a blue fleece pullover, his first public appearance in anything save an orange prison jumpsuit for close to two years since his arrest. His head was shaved, his voice was deep and grumbling. He now had a stocky build, a far cry from the skinny scared kid of two years before, and his skin was paled by the seasons of incarceration.

Cohron began his direct examination by trying to establish a friendship between Stephen and Luke, that they could very well have been partners in crime.

"How long have you known Lucas Goodrum?" Cohron asked.

"Pretty much all my life. He was good friends with my brother back all the way through school and stuff."

"Before May of 2003, had you ever done anything socially before with Mr. Goodrum?"

"Yes. I've stayed at his dad's house and everything. We was kind of friends, you could say."

Stephen calmly retold the story of going back to Katie's room, Luke's clandestine appearance, and her brutal attack. He explained lying to Pickett about his involvement. "I got kind of scared, you know, what was going on. I didn't want nothin' to happen to me and my family by me talking to the police or anything."

After a break, it was time for the defense to question Soules. His demeanor became more guarded and his disdain was thinly masked. Stephen rhythmically swiveled in his chair.

"Do you have any reason to explain how Lucas Goodrum would have known you were in Hugh Poland Hall in room 214?" Broderick asked.

"No sir, and I'm still not aware of that."

"Did Possum tell him?"

"That's the only person that knew where I was. And after I talked to her roommate, those are the only two people that knew where I was at."

"He just appeared?"

"I don't know how he knew where I was at."

"It's fair to say you have not given the same version of what you say took place on early morning May 4, 2003, at any one time. You've given different stories, haven't you?" Broderick asked, preparing the jury for the videotaped interviews to be screened.

"Yes, sir, because I was scared of the threats that was made towards me and my family, and I wasn't sure what I was going to do at that time."

The lights were dimmed, and a television was wheeled out on a metal stand into the court. On the screen was a very different Stephen Soules than the one sitting on the witness stand. The Stephen on the monitor was two years younger, twenty years old but looked sixteen. He was lanky, with neat black hair. In contrast to his sullen boldness on the stand, he was cowering. The jury watched Stephen's widely varied accounts of the crime, and the effect was powerful. The discrepancies piled up, and much of what he said challenged common sense.

The defense presented two confiscated letters giving two other accounts of what happened in room 214, with other varying details.

Stephen was instructed to read from the passages. After much back-and-forth, he finally agreed after the originals were produced that they were in his handwriting.

Stephen had written that during Katie's attack, "I went in to my own world and was prayin' for her and me."

Stephen said that the pages were written to make the guards feel stupid if they searched his cell.

"This letter is a lie?"

"That's what I said."

"You've told a lot of lies, haven't you?"

"No. I was just scared to tell the truth because of the threats that was made towards me."

"Well, now at that point in time—this was written in July of 2003, and so that's after you know Lucas is in jail? And in fact, you knew on May 12th when you gave the statement to Detective Pickett that Lucas was in jail, didn't you?"

"Yeah."

"You've also told the ladies and gentlemen of the jury that before—according to your story—before Lucas got to room 214 in Hugh Poland Hall, you stole the jewelry?"

"Yeah."

"So, and this is a young lady you just met. She's been

passionate with you and you've gone to her room and when she leaves the room, you steal from her. That's the kind of guy you are?"

"Well, you know, people make mistakes, you know."

"Even though you've been drinking and doing drugs all day, one of the first things you thought about was stealing from her. Is that correct?"

"I'm not proud of it."

"Have you ever told anybody that Lucas made you steal the jewelry?"

"Well, like at first I didn't tell the truth, you know what I'm saying, because I was scared. And I believe I did tell Detective Pickett on one occasion at my granmama's, yes."

"But in your letter of July 30th, 2003, you say he made you take the jewelry?"

"Yes, sir. It's just to keep people from going through my stuff. It was like if somebody was looking through my stuff, you know what I'm saying, and they found it and they turned it in, they would look pretty dumb. You know what I'm saying?"

Broderick went on to ask Stephen about the ample size of his brother and father to undermine the claim that he felt threatened. Finally, he is asked if it was true that he said that he felt like a victim.

"Yes, and I still feel that way."

CHAPTER 4

Whatever interaction there was between the families of Katie, Luke, and Stephen was mostly wordless. But there was one striking encounter between Donna Dugas and Shirley Inman. During a break, the two convened in the hallway outside the courtroom. They shared a tearful embrace; they were unmoving, surrounded by the swirl of people walking to the restrooms or the water fountains or outside for a cigarette. Donna told Shirley that she was sorry for her loss and that she couldn't imagine the loss of a child and that she would pray. Shirley responded that she would do the same.

On March 11, Danica Jackson's mother, Donna Jackson, also made her final attempt at communication with Virginia White. Donna had come to take her daughter to trial to testify. During a break in testimony, Donna saw Virginia in the hallway of the courthouse.

"I have wanted so many times to reach out to the aunt," Donna Jackson recalled. "I was thinking this has got to be costing them a lot of money to have to come here to Owensboro from Morgantown. And I know they don't have much money anyway. And I went up to her, and I was gonna give her some money. I said, 'Here, I want you to take this because I know it's costing you a lot of money to be here.' She wouldn't take it."

During lunch the Autrys sat chain-smoking next to the soda machine, while the Goodrums went to the back to dine with Luke, ordering from the nicest restaurant in town. Luke ate a club sandwich each day. Over their meal, Luke's legal team and family reviewed what had transpired that day and strategized the next step in their game plan.

One day when the jury was excused after testimony, Broderick played some of Stephen Soules and Aaron Marr's homemade raps to have in the court record since Judge Castlen declared them inadmissible.

In one song Stephen rapped, "What I'm saying, dawg, we street survivors as we rolling by getting high to the motherfucking sky and it ain't no thang to have yo bitch sucking my dick with another bitch suck on my ass, 'cause I'm a pimp-ass nigga I get yo bitch to toss my motherfucking salad, it ain't no thang."

In another, he enthuses, "Fuck her in the butt, fuck her in the cunt, not giving a damn I'll beat her in the fucking brown brown."

Soules and Marr insist that while these lyrics may be seen as inflammatory and sexist, they aren't a key to anything. They were just aping a popular genre of hip-hop.

Designated driver Ryan "Possum" Payne's testimony was useless to the prosecution and the defense. The last person to see Katie and Stephen together before chauffeuring Luke to his car, Possum claimed a total lack of recollection of the details.

Possum, balding and aged beyond his twenty-three years, wore a red plaid flannel shirt and a wheat-colored barn jacket.

Mike Pearson asked, "When you were taking Katie and Stephen in the truck, do you recall any conversation between Katie and Stephen?"

"No, sir."

All of Payne's responses were clipped. His answers were military-like in their brevity, immediateness, and use of "sir." Considering that he was the one sober person at the party, his memory was remarkably poor.

"Don't recall them saying anything at all?"

"No, sir."

"You don't recall her making a joke about him getting sick and calling him 'Sick Boy'?"

"No, sir."

"Do you recall any kind of interaction between them, them starting to kiss or grope around a little bit?"

"No, sir."

"Don't remember that happening and telling them they ought to knock that off?"

"No, sir."

"No conversation, no fooling around?"

"No, sir."

"Do you not remember any conversation between you and Stephen about him wanting to go back and check on Katie?"

"No, sir."

"And about you letting him off not at Bemis but up the drive a little bit and him walking back towards—"

Before Pearson could finish his question, Payne blurted out, "No, sir."

Pearson continued with his questioning.

"You don't remember any conversation between Katie and Stephen while you were giving them a ride?"

"No, sir."

Broderick objected, "Your Honor, that question has been asked and answered."

The attorneys approached the bench. The gentle static of white noise was played over the speakers so the jury couldn't hear their conversation.

"I would like to go through cumulative what he says he doesn't remember," Pearson told the judge fiercely. "I'd like to go through in detail all these things—this litany of things that he said he doesn't remember."

"I'll permit it," Castlen told him. "I just don't want to get into asking the same question over and over."

The attorneys left the bench.

"While they were in your truck, you don't remember any conversation between Katie and Stephen?" Pearson asked Payne again.

Like a mantra, Payne responded, "No, sir."

A notable character witness for the defense was Mitch Carter, a twenty-year-old acquaintance of Stephen Soules who had known him since seventh grade. Carter alleged that in 2002 Soules stole a truck and then set it on fire and rolled it down a hill. His testimony lent credence to the possibility that Soules had a predilection for starting fires.

The defense called a procession of high-profile experts. Each was well paid to appear and their credentials were flaunted.

First up was James O. Ingram, a retired FBI agent who once ran the New York FBI office, before becoming deputy assistant director of criminal investigations in D.C. (which put him among the top twenty officials in the FBI), then headed their Chicago office. He worked on the investigation into the assassination of the Reverend Martin Luther King, Jr., and was the inspiration for Gene Hackman's character in the film *Mississippi Burning*.

Ingram offered the idea that a second accomplice was involved in the crime was suggested by Detective Kevin Pickett during the interrogation. "When Soules was first asked he mentioned that he felt it was the victim's boyfriend that had committed the act. Then the second time asked, it was a dude in the hallway, and then when it was suggested it was another person, a buddy. And that's when I believe in my opinion that Soules knew that was a bluff, he knew the facts, he knew what happened, and he grabbed this and ran with it to enter another person, and then that would limit his involvement, per se, in this."

Next up for the defense was Tim Palmbach, an associate professor and the director of forensic science for the University of New Haven, and a former member of the Connecticut State Police and Department of Public Safety. He coauthored *Henry Lee's Crime Scene Handbook* with Dr. Henry Lee, the preeminent forensic scientist turned crime scene superstar due to his testimony at the O. J. Simpson trial.

Palmbach introduced and explained Locard's theory to the Court. Locard's theory states that a perpetrator of a crime will always both bring something into the scene and leave with something from the scene. Upon cross-examination, Pearson raised the possibility of water washing away evidence.

"But water is not going to wash away selectively only one suspect's hair," Palmbach replied.

Pearson countered that fire could have also destroyed evidence.

A tense moment occurred when Palmbach accidentally referred to Katie as "Katie Soules" during questioning.

Virginia White's stern voice loudly erupted from the audience in the middle of Palmbach's testimony. "Hello, her name is Katie Autry!"

CHAPTER 5

Broderick's examination of WKU Police Chief Robert Deane was particularly detrimental to the prosecution's case. The head of the WKU police force, the person responsible for the decision that WKU take control of the investigation, Deane had not even been called by the Commonwealth as a prosecution witness. Deane sat in the witness stand in a blue suit, his hair a distinguished gray. He carried himself confidently, and his Michigan accent was striking compared to the Kentuckians who had taken the stand up until that point.

The defense began by questioning Deane's decision to take over the investigation.

"And it was based at the time on the fact that you knew both of the people that would be the investigators had no experience in investigating homicides?"

"No, I would not agree with that."

"Well, what experience did they have?"

"They didn't have any experience, but that did not—"

"That didn't play a factor at all in your decision?"

"No, it did not."

"Were you aware that Detective Dowell had never worked a homicide investigation?"

"Yes, I was."

"At the time that you came to Western in 2000—from 2000 to May 4th of 2003, did Detective Dowell receive any training in arson investigation?"

"None formal, no."

"Well, had Western had any arsons from 2000 to May 4th, 2003?"

"Not that I can recall, no, sir."

"The reason I was asking you is you mentioned on-the-job training, and I just wanted to make sure there wasn't a situation there. Had you had any rape cases on Western's campus from 2000 to May 4th, 2003?"

"Yes, we have. Let me clarify that. Allegations of rape, but no formal full-scale investigation."

"Were there any charges?"

"No, not that I can recall."

"So at this point when Western took over the investigation based on your decision, the investigators you had had no homicide experience, no arson experience, no experience in rape. Is that correct?"

"Yes."

There was an audible murmur in the courtroom. Broderick paused to begin another line of questioning.

"In your experience, on-the-job training as a police officer and both now as a police officer and as an administrator of police officers, is it a good police practice to check out a suspect's alibi witness?"

"Yes, it is."

"It is one of the main things you need to do to rule in or rule out whether somebody's done something, isn't it?"

"I don't know if it's one of the main things, but it's something that should be done."

"If somebody does not check out alibi witnesses as a law enforcement official in investigating a homicide, based upon your training and experience, they haven't done a complete job, have they?"

"That's correct."

"I want to take you now to May 10th, 2003. Let me put this in perspective. May 10th is a Saturday. On May 10th, we have heard testimony in this case, we have seen videotapes in this case, where Stephen Soules has given two statements that day. Would it be a fair statement to say that immediately after Lucas Goodrum gave his statement, or maybe even a little bit before he was through, but somewhere in the time period while you were at the state police lab, a decision was made to arrest Lucas Goodrum on the spot, wasn't it?"

"That's correct."

"Who made that decision?"

"I made that decision."

"And you made that decision without the benefit of checking out his alibi witnesses, didn't you?"

"That's correct."

"Is it fair to say you made that decision solely on the statements of Stephen Soules?"

"Yes."

"Was it based on anything else other than Stephen Soules?"

"Yes. In my estimation, Goodrum presented a possibility of flight. He had relatives that lived out of town in Texas. His family was connected with the Dollar General store organization, which gave him the means."

"So now, let's talk about this. May 4th, 2003, is when things took place on Western's campus. And so six days later, May the 10th, is the first time anybody had any contact with Lucas Goodrum. Had he ever left Kentucky in that six-day period of time?"

"Not that I know of."

"Do you know why Lucas Goodrum's alibi witnesses were not interviewed prior to his arrest on May 10th, 2003?"

"No, I do not."

Luke's alibi witnesses, his father and stepmother Judy, were contacted well *after* Luke's arrest. Mike Goodrum was called on July 1, 2003, and Judy Goodrum was called just the week prior to Luke's trial, in fact, in February 2005.

"Certainly that's not good police practice, is it, Chief Deane?"

"Not ideal circumstances, no."

"Chief, is it fair to say that you had contact with the president of Western Kentucky University during this process?"

"Yes."

"This was a matter of great concern on Western's campus, was it not, sir?"

"Certainly."

"You all were in a hurry to solve this, weren't you?"

"That would be a fair representation, yes."

Broderick had no more questions. The Commonwealth had none at all for the chief of Western police, and Deane stepped down from the stand.

CHAPTER 6

Despite the interrogation videos, Luke's voice was still a surprise to the spectators when he took the stand on the morning of March 16, 2005—the heavy accent, the speed of his cadence. He wore a blue shirt, a navy blazer with gold buttons, and a blue tie. Luke retold a similar story to what he told Pickett during his interrogation. He added new details to his history of the night, though.

Luke told of a pit stop at a Citgo near Franklin.

"I stopped at a gas station to get a Sprite and I had to get a couple of dollars' worth of gas in my Mustang." Luke testified that he paid in cash, and then arrived at his father's house at approximately 3 AM.

"My dad had to talk to me about me not having a job. The incident that happened that night with my girlfriend, the argument me and her had, about Ed Stinson, he had called and that worried me a lot. We talked for about thirty or forty-five minutes." Luke also stated that his stepmother, Judy Goodrum, was present for this exchange. Luke said that his father offered him a place to stay until morning in one of the extra bedrooms, but that he went to his car to sleep instead. Luke said he awoke with the sunrise and returned to the apartment he shared with Matt Hire at around 7 AM.

Broderick and his client delved into the peculiar matter of sleeping in the closet. Luke testified that he stayed in for three hours, not three days, and this was because of a fear of Ed Stinson returning. Luke claimed that he thought he was picked up by the police solely because of the altercation with Brittany. Luke stated that he never told any of the prison snitches anything, and in fact had no recollection of ever meeting Micah West.

Furthermore, one constant in each of Stephen Soules's fluid retellings was that Luke was not in room 214 during Danica Jackson's phone call.

Cohron began his cross-examination trying to establish that Stephen and Luke were friends, not just acquaintances. He pointed out that Luke used the term "friends" in his interrogation with Pickett. Luke countered that he was an "acquaintance," but that that term just wouldn't come up in everyday parlance. Cohron flipped through the transcript and read aloud each time he used "friend." Cohron would make a lot of this difference between "friend" and "acquaintance," and throughout Luke's questioning with the prosecution, words and their exact meaning and usage were continually examined.

Cohron took a tone of barely masked anger when he asked Luke why he went to his father's house instead of his own apartment.

"Because where I live at by the ballpark," Luke explained, "you've got to go past Jr. Foods. And there ain't many places in a little town like Scottsville that stayed open twenty-four hours. And I would say about from twelve to five in the morning there's always cops sitting there. And they had been by my apartment that night so I didn't think it wise for me to have to go by that gas station and them to see my car or hear my car because the cops knew what my car looked like. So my dad lived on Franklin Road, I was tired, so I just went and stopped at my dad's house."

The questioning then led to the incident with Brittany.

"Well, you hit Brittany?"

"I did not hit Brittany," Luke said, adding, "I slapped Brittany. It was foolish. It was childish on my part. It was just something that I shouldn't have done. I got angry because me and her got in a slapping contest. I mean, she slapped me, I slapped her. That was basically the extent of it. I was fully wrong, you know, and Mr. Stinson come the next night and straightened me up and, you know, let me know that that would never happen again."

"So when you say you don't hit women you mean you don't"—Cohron interrupted his question to illustrate it by hitting the palm of his hand, which made a loud smack throughout the courtroom—"punch them?"

"No, sir."

"You don't hit them like a guy hits a guy?"

"No, sir."

"But it's okay to slap women?"

"No, it's not okay to slap women."

"Well, now, you slapped Katie Autry in her dorm room?" Cohron countered.

"No, sir, I did not."

"Well, you had already slapped one woman that night?"

"If you mean Brittany, yes, sir."

"So, it's okay to slap Brittany, but not—"

Lucas interjected sternly, "I believe I just stated that it's not all right. I don't condone that kind of thing. It's not right."

Cohron directed the discussion to Luke's alibi. He said sarcastically, "It's awful convenient that the night you're accused, your parents are your alibi. Thank God you went to your dad's house."

"I'm sitting up here stating the truth," Luke reponded, flustered. "That's all I am here doing. I'm testifying to the truth of what happened that night I'm accused of some heinous crime that I did not have nothing to do with!"

Broderick's closing statement reiterated the defense's theory that the investigation was deeply flawed, that Luke was arrested solely on the word of Stephen Soules, and that once Luke had been apprehended the investigation ceased. Broderick asked the jurors to think about the timeline of the crime and the implausibility of Luke being able to be at Hugh Poland Hall or even knowing what room Katie Autry was in. Broderick emphasized the fact that no evidence was ever found connecting Luke to the crime, and that the sprinklers wouldn't selectively wash away evidence from one suspect.

For his closing argument, Chris Cohron was the most animated and persuasive he had been during the course of the trial.

"An old criminal defense attorney one time was asked, 'How do you defend the undefendable?' He said, 'Smoke and mirrors my friend, smoke and mirrors.' As we've gone through and you've listened to the points made by defense counsel, that's solely what it is."

He wandered the area of the podium.

"First smoke."

Cohron illustrated with a puffing sound and continued, "You've heard the mention of a place called Tattle Tails. They made sure that you heard that. Why? Because they can't call her a whore. They want one of y'all to latch on to that fact to let him walk. Maybe she just deserved it."

Lisa made her only appearance in court that day. Her

resemblance to Katie was startling and there were quiet whispers when she entered. She sat next to Barbie, who was wearing a pink vinyl jacket. Barbie held her and the jacket made a crinkling sound when they moved. Lisa only lasted in the courtroom about ten minutes before erupting in uncontrolled anguish. She left hurriedly and Barbie followed her.

Cohron asked the jury to remember that Luke used the word "friend" to describe Stephen. He reminded them that the sprinkler had been on for thirty-five minutes and that the primary crime scene was Katie herself, ergo no evidence could be found of Luke.

He finished by saying, "You've had to listen to witnesses, some of which as we've heard are convicted felons. Ladies and gentlemen, as you go back to the jury room to deliberate, I leave you with this. Sometimes to convict the devil, you have to go to hell to get your witnesses and that's what we've had to do. We've provided every fact to you we knew. It's now time to return a verdict of guilty."

CHAPTER 7

The jury reached a verdict after less than three hours of deliberation. Court reconvened in anticipation and the foreman passed the verdict to Judge Castlen, who read all the counts of the indictment aloud with the same decision after each: not guilty.

During Castlen's recital, loud murmuring spread throughout the audience. "Quiet, please!" a bailiff shouted.

After the first "not guilty" was read, Luke knew that the rest of the counts would also come out in his favor. He made the sign of the cross on his chest and then dabbed his tears with a wadded tissue.

Weeping of a very different sort burst out in the two halves of the courtroom. The first law of thermodynamics is that the total energy of the universe remains constant—energy can neither be created nor destroyed. There was a transfer of energy between the two families. The Goodrum side of the courtroom radiated euphoria like sunbeams. A force was being pushed out from them, a jubilation that could physically be felt around them like a wave.

"We're taking him home!" Bruce Dugas told Donna as he hugged her.

The Autrys collapsed into one another with a howl. It was like a gravitational core suddenly pulled them together. The kinetic motion and frenzy of the Goodrum-Dugas side of the room was contrasted by the eerie stillness of the women huddled into a ball.

Luke would have to be taken back and processed, but he would soon be officially released.

Donna Dugas wiped her eyes and marched triumphantly out of the courtroom. When she got to the elevator, Cohron and Pearson were already on it. A friend advised her not to get on with them.

"Why not?" Donna asked, adding, "They took two years of my son's life, they can put up with me for a ride on the elevator."

Donna got on with them and after the doors closed, she said, "Well boys, you didn't accomplish what ya wanted, did ya? I'm waitin' on an apology."

The rest of the descent was completely silent.

"I had been there that morning," Barbie says, "and Lisa had had a panic attack and so I had brought her home and put her to bed. When the verdict was read I was sittin' in the living room. Katie's mother was sittin' in the bedroom watchin' soap operas and it come across the bottom of the TV and she hollered. I went back there. She was lookin' at the TV and I seen it goin' across the bottom. I freaked out. I just went into panics and started crying and I couldn't even stand up. I don't see how he got away with it.

"Me and Lisa got in my car and drove around for hours," she continues. "Just me and her. We didn't want to see nobody. We just wanted to be together and alone." The pair roamed the winding roads in silence.

* * *

A brief press conference was held at the Executive Inn immediately upon Luke's release. Luke sat surrounded by his family and defense team, all wearing "Lucas Is Innocent" buttons, in front of a throng of reporters and television cameras.

"I knew the truth would prevail," Luke said into the microphone. "I mean, it had to. After two years of being wrongfully jailed, I'm happy to be a free man and be able to be with my family."

He added, "I ain't going to hold no harsh feelings toward the state of Kentucky or nobody."

What Luke said wasn't particularly what was on his mind. "The dude that always did the reporting on my case at WKBO," Luke says, "I wanted to say 'Fuck you' to him. I didn't even want him asking me a question. They asked me how I feel about Soules and all that stuff, and I said, 'I really hold no grudges against him.' And that was a fucking lie. They told me to keep it simple and everything, but I just got out of jail, I didn't want to say nothing to piss anybody off because I thought they was gonna throw me back in. Hell yeah, I was mad, but I tried to cover up and basically say what they told me to say. But there was a lot of stuff I wanted to say about Soules and the district attorney, Cohron, and the whole situation. It was fucked up and I would have liked to have said more words about how it was fucked up. I was hoping that Stephen Soules got the death penalty. That's what I think he should have got and they made a deal with the devil basically. That wasn't really what I wanted to say. I should have said what I wanted to say when they asked me all those questions. I wanted to say how angry I was at the justice system. How could they do that to a person? I wanted to know."

After the press conference, Luke and his mother left Owensboro. Luke didn't feel like driving all night to Texas. They decided to return to Scottsville to stay at their lake house and an intimate celebration was planned. They stopped into McDonald's for dinner. Luke had his cap pulled down and no one recognized him.

Some friends of the family came by and two of Luke's high school buddies. "We got fucked up," he says. "It didn't take a lot, I just drank two or three beers and I was drunk. I got to eat good McDonald's and get drunk with a couple of my friends."

Early the next morning, Luke and his mother left Kentucky for the twelve-hour drive to Texas.

CHAPTER 8

On May 12, 2005, Stephen Soules was officially sentenced. Soules, again in his orange prison jumpsuit, his wrists handcuffed in front of him, sat next to his public defenders, Renae Tuck and George Sornberger, in a Bowling Green courtroom. Cohron and Dowell, looking particularly dour and defeated, sat at the other table representing the Commonwealth. Judge Castlen entered and those present rose for the proceedings.

Soules had signed a plea for life without parole in 2004, but the judge still had the power to alter this arrangement and could give Stephen the chance for lighter sentencing. Many friends and family members had sent Judge Castlen letters pleading for leniency for Stephen. They had as much of a problem attributing responsibility to Stephen as he had to himself.

An aunt had written, "had the jury heard of Goodrum's abuse of women, even as far back as high school, the verdict may have been different. He truly masterminded the series of events that came to such a tragic end for Miss Autry. I truly feel my Stephen was also a victim in that dorm room."

Another aunt opined, "I believe my nephew when he told me he did not cause Miss Autry's death. He would never hurt anyone. He came forward with information because he was undeniably there with her. He was not a coconspirator in her murder. Sadly, I feel the real murderer was acquitted."

In the audience facing the judge's bench, the Soules family had assembled and filled their half. Many of the cousins had gotten out of school to attend. It was a gathering of all ages, from the smallest cousin up to the matriarch, Evangeline, who was there for her favorite grandchild.

Across the aisle, the left side of the courtroom was almost empty. Virginia, Barbie, and Lisa were completely alone save for a smattering of reporters around the outer perimeter. Virginia had met alone with Stephen before the sentencing.

"I asked permission to see Stephen Soules," she said. "I don't know what I expected. It was just something I felt like I needed to do. He kept apologizing saying he didn't know what to say, that he regretted what had happened. In my opinion, in his mind he didn't see his participation in it as actually hurting Katie."

In the courtroom, Stephen awkwardly raised his restrained hands to wipe the tears streaming down his face. The polished steel of the handcuffs gleamed. Stephen was silently weeping, there were no sounds or convulsions, just the steady stream of tears.

Sornberger, a large man in a gray suit in his midfifties, looked like a typical attorney, but his balding gray hair was greased back into a small ponytail. He stood to speak for his client.

"I ask you, Judge, to think about what Stephen has

done since he made the decision to admit responsibility for his involvement," said Sornberger. "He's told the truth. He's cooperated with the authorities. He's testified truthfully and to the best of his ability. He's expressed remorse and he's been held to answer for his involvement. I don't know what else we could have asked of this young man under these circumstances. Judge, I think that never could doing so little count for so much, and that's simply to take your pen on the papers that are before you and letter in 'twenty-five' after the life without the possibility of parole."

Stephen craned his neck and wiped tears on his shoulder, the orange of the jumpsuit darkening subtly with the moisture.

"To simply add those numbers, Judge," Sornberger continued, "allows this twenty-two-year-old young man to live with at least a *possibility* of the hope that someday he might meet the parole board and they might see fit to parole him. You have the power to temper this seeming injustice. Are we so afraid to have somebody in a position of authority take a look at Stephen's situation in twenty-five years? I don't think so. Because I don't know if I'm going to be here, I hope all of us in this room are going to be—"

Judge Castlen cut him off and interjected, "But we certainly know Katie Autry won't be here."

It was Stephen's turn, and he walked up to the podium.

"Judge, this hasn't been easy on none of us, you know," Stephen said. "I've seen a lot of pain involved around this case, you know, with my family and with Miss Autry's family as well. I'd just like to apologize for my involvement in what happened and I'm sorry for all the pain I've caused anyone surrounding this case and I'm sorry for everything that happened that night, you know, Judge. I just feel that if . . ."

Stephen paused and then rapidly continued, "It's not all my fault, Judge. And I ask that you just please just search yourself and maybe if you overturn my sentence or if you don't, it's all the will of God that's going to happen here today, you know. I'm just here to say 'I'm sorry' to Miss Autry and her family."

He motioned at them with his head and went on: "I'm sorry for every tear that they've cried over Katie, you know. But you know, the Lord has blessed me with the chance to still live, you know. I might still spend life in prison, you know, but I'm still alive, you know, and that's far more than I can say for Miss Autry, and I'm sorry for that, you know. And now, you know, I'm looking at life without parole, and I still try to find the good in every situation, you know, and I'm sorry for what Katie and her family have been through. And I know it's been very hard and I know that my sorrys won't bring her back, but I would just like for her family to know I'm sorry and I hope that one day they can forgive me for my involvement in the case."

Stephen took a seat and his father, Danny Soules, stepped up to speak, wearing a brown polo shirt tucked neatly into slacks.

"Your honor, I come with a plea of mercy upon the court. My prayer is that my son may have the hope of returning to civilization. I think it is very unfair to get everything dumped upon you just because you're man enough to admit your guilt. This is a horrendous crime. This is definitely not Stephen Soules's character. I know that he couldn't have done this by himself. There was a lot of things that should have come out in this trial that never made it. Mr. Goodrum was made to look like the perfect altar boy. Stephen was made to look like the hardest criminal you ever seen. And I know my family's not rich and we have limited resources. When you're up against unlimited resources you don't have a chance."

Danny's world-weary voice gained rhythm, clarity, and confidence as he spoke. He didn't prepare his speech beforehand, but it flowed without cessation. Behind him was the vast Soules clan in their Sunday best. Their heads were all uniformly bowed as if in prayer, and the rows of plastic chairs at the Warren County Justice Center were for the moment just like the pews at the First Baptist Church in Scottsville. Danny emphasized his points by raising and lowering his left hand like a revival preacher.

"The truth may not happen down here. But one day, true judgment will come! Money won't be able to buy it. There won't be no money collectors at this gate! There's a lot of things that I feel that just not right. But I'll leave that alone because I know the Autry family, I know that they're hurt. They've got a scar on them for the rest of their life. I'll plea for my son's life in a penitentiary. I'll still get a chance to see him, I'll still talk to him and they don't have that. That deeply saddens me. It's every parent's obligation to look out for a child. I have to do this, this is something my heart tells me to do. And as a parent it's hard. I hope no one else has to stand in the shoes that the Autry family is standing in and the Soules family. I'll leave the Goodrum family out of this because they're standing on shaky ground. Our feet are on solid. This was all a game to them. The seriousness was took out. But that was a young lady that lost her life, there's a family that's going to forever grieve. There's another family that lost their son, they can't see him, he's not in their household no more. They can't touch him. He can't be there when they need him, but at least he is still alive. And I also want to apologize to the Autry family."

Danny turned and faced Virginia, Barbie, and Lisa.

"This was very devastating for y'all," he said, his voice downshifting to a soothing tone. "But my prayers will always be with y'all forever. I see your faces, I see the hurt and I see the pain. I know it's hard right now, as time goes on, God will heal you and he will help you in your heart. Katie walks in heaven with God right now. And she still thinks of you just like y'all still think of her. And as long as she's in your heart, she's not gone, she always will be fine."

Danny faced the judge again and bowed slightly and said clearly into the microphone, "Thank you, Your Honor. Thank you, the court."

Danny's discourse was a mixture of the convincing and the heartfelt, but also the ill-informed, with its references to an undefined unfairness. Either he failed to perceive or refused to believe that Stephen could have gone to trial himself, and its constant blame on someone else for Stephen's admitted actions. Danny and Stephen repeatedly implied that there was some kind of injustice in his sentence. But even if everything had unfolded exactly as Stephen had said in one of the myriad and varying ways he retold it, Soules was still admittedly part of a murder, rape, and arson. Still, it was the *way* that Danny gave his impassioned plea that made it so potent. His comportment was solid: he could withstand a gale—at least from the waist up. What was only visible from behind the stand was the terrified trembling of his legs.

It was now time for Katie's family to get their say. Lisa was tiny and rail-thin, her hair pulled back in a headband. The podium dwarfed her, but conviction carried her voice.

As she spoke, the power of her words made her appear larger and larger.

"Stephen Soules and his friend took someone I love very much out of my life, my older sister Katie Autry. Stephen Soules, by making this mistake of killing my sister, you have affected your life, but you have also affected mine. She will not be there on my wedding day or see my future children grow up. That's my only dream as a kid, to have my big sister there by my side. Because of your cowardness my dreams are shattered. Your family can see you in prison. Me and my mother can only see Katie through pictures and at the cemetery, where she is laying six feet under because of you. In life I hope that I can finally get some closure from my sister's death but until then I hope that you rot in prison. You and your family may think that Katie was nothing or nobody, but to me she was my everything. She was my mother figure, my best friend, and my big Sissie, and she's a girl that could have accomplished anything in life but I will never know where her life would have taken her thanks to you, *Sick Boy*."

Lisa spit the moniker with icy venom, the nickname that Soules claimed Katie had given him in that drive from the Pike party to her dorm room.

Lisa's speech was the most resonant of all those who had their say. When she finished, she retreated back to Virginia and Barbie and collapsed into their embrace. Their huddled stance was reminiscent of when Luke's verdict had been read.

Lisa sobbed audibly in the background as Cohron said, "Mr. Soules has lived up to his end of the bargain. He did testify. We believe he testified truthfully."

"One person we haven't heard from," Judge Castlen

said, "is, of course, Katie Autry. Her lips are sealed, and Mr. Soules, you saw to that."

Stephen Soules was sentenced to life imprisonment with no possibility of parole.

CHAPTER 9

There is a humbling sense of enormity to the vast expanse of Aubrey, Texas. Dusty fields go on for miles and miles, as far as the eye can see, before dropping off at the distant horizon. The sun beats down and tumbleweeds blow across the dirt tracts. It is boundless here, about as opposite as a place can be from jail.

The Double D ranch consists of a modernized main house, a beautiful, stately, green and white horse barn, and a smattering of smaller houses arranged far away from one another on the acreage. Near the main house is a swimming pool fed by a bubbling waterfall, an oasis among the parched vegetation.

Not long after Luke's return, he was joined by his ex-wife, LaDonna (who had divorced her second husband), and Tyler. This reunion was seen as a bad idea to everyone but Luke and LaDonna. "That was the only way I got to see my little boy for such a long period of time," Luke muses. "And shit, she had to come, too. And shit, I been in jail for two years. I'm a man and I needed a woman and I knew I could get that stuff."

It didn't help that the two weren't beginning anew on

untainted soil. Not only was there all the underlying turmoil lingering from their failed marriage, but Luke also
had not forgiven LaDonna for not visiting him in jail.
Unsurprisingly, their renewed union was soon in tatters
and LaDonna returned to Kentucky.

It is the fall of 2006, and Luke now has a different Brittany in his life. They met when he stopped into the store
to buy some cat food and the eighteen-year-old was working there. Her parents can't stand him, and that was true
even before her father found out that Luke had been Kentucky's most famous murder suspect of the decade. Brittany's father had a background check done and learned
that Luke had already been divorced.

Luke and Brittany live in a separate house on the ranch
property. He drives a Mule, a rugged four-wheeler, to get
from the main house to his modest one-story wooden cottage with a green-shingled roof. The porch is stacked
with firewood, a swinging bench, and random debris like
plastic gasoline jugs and soda bottles. Off to the side is a
deflated camping tent, and mismatched lawn chairs circle
a stone-ringed fire pit. Behind the dwelling are dark, gap-
ing woods. The trees are barren, dried out by years of
unrelenting sun. In the forest is a sharp incline that leads
treacherously down to a gulley. Luke has practiced de-
scending the steep hill in the four-wheeler in case he finds
himself in need of an escape route.

Inside, the house looks as if a search warrant has been
executed. Clothes are piled in mountains and no surface
is left uncovered. A *Scarface* movie poster, neon boogie
boards, and framed family photos crowd the walls. Pizza
boxes, fast-food drink cups, and other refuse is piled on
the counter.

Luke has been working at the ranch. When he first got

back, he would watch the sun come up because he couldn't sleep. He would mow the fields at 2 AM with the tractor until he was so tired he could collapse in bed. The sleep that finally came to him was rough and rife with nightmares. The door and windows all had to be open or else it would feel as if the room were collapsing around him, the atmosphere suffocating.

But there are moments of pure joy when he goes outside in the early morning. He can often be found playing with the dogs in the driveway.

"Isn't it gorgeous today?" he asked his mother one day. "Look how green the trees are, look how bright that sun is." He had never noticed these things before.

Luke spends a lot of time with his girlfriend and he also has old friends in town. Sometimes, to pass the time, he and his buddies go back into the woods and shoot coyotes with AK-47s. He plays basketball up by the main house and practices golf in a clearing he has mowed. The back room of his house has been converted to a weight room and he is trying to get back into shape. He also watches his large-screen television a lot and is sure to catch *General Hospital* every day.

Luke is happy remaining under the watchful eye of his mother. Luke and his mother go on late-night motorcycle rides through the back roads behind the house, yelling to each other over the din of the engines.

Luke gets in the Mule ATV and drives out onto the ranch. He speeds to a gate and hurriedly hops out of the seat to unlatch and open it. He steers into the middle of a field that holds about fifty horses and turns off the noisy vehicle.

The horses are beautiful, tall and powerful, and the sheer number of them is dizzying. Curious, they slowly sidle up from all directions in unison and surround the four-wheeler.

"These are all brood mares," Luke says. "I really only rode them once. They're like a person, they can think for themselves and they can buck my ass anytime. I used to cut all this as hay until they put the horses in here. That's ten dollars a bale, especially during the wintertime."

Life on the ranch allows Luke plenty of time to reflect on his incarceration.

"I wasn't a great kid," he says. "I was always doin' drugs and dealin' drugs and getting fucked up on coke and X. I think it was karma for how I treated women. I was an asshole. It was a big eye-opener."

CHAPTER 10

It is an unseasonably hot early March in 2007. It's as if winter has gone directly to summer and bypassed spring. It is T-shirt weather; the sun is shining brightly and the sky is crystalline azure. Morgantown is only about a twenty-five-minute drive north on the parkway from Bowling Green, but as one progresses up the parkway it's as if you are crossing into another climatic zone. Rapidly, the sky turns pale violet, then gray, then black. Flakes of snow rain down like volcanic ash.

The sign greeting visitors to Morgantown reads THE BUSIEST LITTLE TOWN IN KENTUCKY, which doesn't seem particularly apt. Up a gravel road near the plastic factory is the double-wide trailer that is home to the Whites. Down the road is a large Dollar General store that must seem like a memento mori to the family.

At Virginia's residence, the sun is trying to return. Clouds block it, but there is now a brightness to the sky. It is no longer blue, but neither is it black. The color has been washed away altogether and it is a pale soft white. Intermittent bursts of snow spit down and interrupt the rays.

Inside, Virginia, Donnie, Lisa, and Barbie sit around

the kitchen table. On the table is Virginia's pack of Marlboro 100 cigarettes in a worn leather pouch with a silver snap-buckle. She lights one, languidly exhales, and the smoke joins the ample cloud from the rest of the women. Virginia reaches for her coffee that's in a clear juice glass—there is always a pot of coffee ready at the White household and Virginia drinks it liberally, black and strong, throughout the day. Virginia's youngest daughter, a precocious strawberry-blonde tomboy, Lil' Johnni, is playing in the living room. On the windowsill next to the brown overstuffed couch is a drooping fern in a blue plastic pot with "Katie" painted on the rim. Donnie has a distance to her, a gaze that just doesn't quite meet you. She will voice opinions at random intervals in a squawky, thickly accented Kentucky brogue. "You make me nervous," she will say and shyly clasp her hand over her mouth, shielding her teeth in front of a newcomer—she is missing quite a few. Her hair is light, thin, and soft, and set around her head in a halo. Donnie's chair is positioned close to Lisa's, and they are leaning on each other.

Lisa's hair is dyed a deep chestnut. It makes her skin look paler, smoother. It is long and straightened and hangs below her shoulders. Dark liner circles her eyes. She looks lovely. In her nostril is a tiny gold stud just like her cousin Barbie's.

Barbie, age twenty-one, wears a long chocolate-brown cardigan that brushes her knees. She is pregnant and the unbuttoned sweater frames her protruding belly. She is expecting a boy, and is going to name him "Kaler" after Katie. Barbie is no longer with the father and that is just fine by her.

"The only boy I need is in my belly," Barbie says, rubbing her stomach with one hand and inhaling from her cigarette with the other.

Virginia is ecstatic to be a grandmother and loves to show off Barbie's ultrasound images.

Lisa moves from the living room out to the wooden back porch and stares out lackadaisically. Poo, a tiny mixed-breed miniature Doberman, energetically skips around Lisa's ankles. Poo's chain connects to a spike in the ground and makes a tinny, rattling sound. Elbows on her knees, Lisa rests her head upon her hands and ignores him.

"I want to go back to school," she says. "When Katie was alive she always told me to follow my dreams and I've been putting my dreams on hold for her. I've been doing what I think Katie would like to do. I was living Katie's life for me, I guess, partying because she did a lot of partying. I used to drink with my cousin. At the parties I didn't talk to nobody. I would just stick by myself. But now it got to the point where I'm going to do what Lisa wants to do."

Lisa hasn't been back to Pellville nor spoken to the Inmans or her old friends. She wants to someday and says she'll know when the time is right, but she's unsure of what her reception will be. She lights a cigarette.

"When I go down to the cemetery," Lisa says, "if I have a cigarette lit, I always put it out."

Katie hated smoking. Katie is buried in Rosine Cemetery, about a mile from where she lived as a little girl. An ever-changing multitude of flowers and small statues of angels and cherubs shroud her grave. OUR PRECIOUS KATIE is carved into the stone, along with an image of a butterfly landing on a rose.

Lisa looks out at the field in front of her. It's covered in the thin skin of the out-of-season snow, pierced here and there with tufts of grass.

"It took a tragedy like this to realize that you love your family," Lisa says. "I guess there was good in it. Although

Katie passed away. Katie knew this is the only way. Katie knew to get us all back together she had to do something. She didn't care if she was happy. She just wanted to see other people happy. It makes me sad to think of Katie dyin' but at the same time I look back on that and that was a turning point because my family was going separate ways, but at that time we had a bond and become one again."

Lisa hasn't been working and spends a lot of time sequestered alone in the apartment she shares with her mother. In her opinion, the most significant change in her life lately is the tattoo she got on her shoulder blade.

"It was the closing chapter," she says. "The tattoo helps me to know she always got my back. She was always there for me. When I'm having a bad day, when I start to cry at home, I just go to the bathroom and I look at my tattoo. For some reason, that helps me stop crying."

The tattoo is of a fairy with butterfly wings. Her arms are outstretched and a butterfly flutters from her open palm. Lisa explains, "The person represents me, and the butterfly represents Katie. I'm letting her go fly away."

EPILOGUE

Although the jury found Lucas Goodrum innocent, the verdict did little if anything to sway the cemented opinion of most Bowling Green and Scottsville residents. This isn't altogether surprising. The public had been conditioned daily for years that Luke was indeed a murderer. His prior history of violence was well documented and broadcast—the jury might not have fully heard about his past, but the public devoured it tenfold. There was barely any public outcry on the mishandling of the case; there was no fury at the authorities. The only staff changes at Western's police force were promotions. Many believed that the miscarriage of justice was that Luke was freed.

"Lucas Goodrum is a monster and I'll always believe that," says Stephen's first attorney, Zach Kafoglis. "I think it's unbelievable that he's on the streets. I don't think Stephen Soules had the intelligence or wherewithal to think of any of the things that were done in this case or even the personality to think of something that heinous."

It became taboo to support Luke Goodrum's innocence. The verdict certainly did not assuage the feelings of Katie's relatives. In many minds, Stephen became something of a martyr. "He's paying for something he didn't do," says one of Stephen's aunts. "He did whatever he felt was going to protect his family. He gave up his life to protect his family."

Despite pleading guilty to murder, rape, sodomy, and arson, and despite DNA evidence linking him to the crime, and Soules's constantly morphing recollection, many of Stephen's family members believe he is innocent and steadfastly stand by him. Two of his cousins and his brother have gotten "Free Guido" tattoos and are planning on making T-shirts with the same slogan.

Some saw Luke as a victim, not of "small town justice," but of the gullibility of Western and its police force. "Maybe at the barrel end of a gun, somebody might coerce you into that crime," says defense attorney Kevin Hackworth. "That was just part of the ludicrousness of Soules's statements that he gave to the police—that he never had a weapon pulled on him or anything like that. It flies in the face of logic that anybody would buy that story. Especially when he was able to leave the room at least, in one of his stories, two different times and he never bothered to leave the scene or try to go make a phone call or anything. The one thing to this day that Stephen Soules can't tell anybody and that the police can't tell anybody is how Lucas Goodrum knew where Katie Autry lived or how Lucas Goodrum knew that Stephen Soules was supposed to be with her. There's no phone records, no witness statement saying that Lucas knew where Katie Autry was. There's nothing."

"Mastermind" is a term that was bandied around frequently in the coverage of the case, in the many dinner conversations it launched, and ultimately in the prosecution of Luke Goodrum. But this term conjures ingenuity and complexity. It doesn't describe Katie's murder, a crime elemental in its crude brutality. This was not the work of an astute evil genius; the trail to Stephen Soules was neon, both in DNA evidence and witnesses. It was made into something more intricate, the thought being that there *had* to be more behind it to cause such destruction and perversion.

Life in Bowling Green went back to normal. Talk of Stephen, Luke, and Katie was no longer conversation fodder. Their faces no longer stared out from newspapers and TV screens.

WKU's football team moved up to Division 1 and would compete at the highest level of college ball. Petitions swirled to fight the looming plans to put a Sonic drive-in next to exit 26, which threatened to ruin the only scenic town entrance not already infested with fast-food franchises. A new Chamber of Commerce building was erected downtown, as was a multimillion-dollar skate park. Life resumed its ordinary path.

Donna and Bruce Dugas's marriage fell apart in late 2005 and they began lengthy divorce proceedings. Luke was at the Double D ranch enjoying his freedom. Stephen had been confined in a medium-security prison, but his incarceration was productive. He got his high school equivalency degree and would soon be moved to a minimum-security facility.

Some of the peripheral players in the story of Katie, Luke, and Stephen overlapped through either small town coincidence or fate. Luke's ex-girlfriend, Brittany, became an in-law of Stephen Soules. She married Valerie Soules's brother.

"I think it's kind of strange that the girl that he whupped that night before this happened is my sister in-law now," Danny says. "It's intertwined."

Brian Moon and Danica Jackson started working at the same restaurant and became friendly. Danny Soules and Virginia White, who officially met at Luke's trial, are still in touch. Aaron Marr and Daniel Soules work at the same factory. They don't really talk to each other, though, as each reminds the other of Stephen.

But in the spring of 2007, after two years of fading into the past, Katie's murder again made headlines. First, on April 19, the Kentucky Supreme Court in Frankfort ruled that Western Kentucky University and the WKU Student Life Foundation are immune from most lawsuits. Virginia and Donnie's personal injury suit, ongoing since September 2003, was dismissed against them. The suit is still pending against the Kentucky Board of Claims. The Autrys can gain a maximum award of $300,000 if the board is found negligent. Bigger news followed less than a week later.

On April 24, an emergency protective order against Luke Goodrum was issued in Franklin by his ex-wife, LaDonna. She wrote on the domestic violence petition: "Lucas called and found out I was getting married and he went off calling me names so I hung up. He called me back telling me he had gun. He shot two rounds and said that he would be in Franklin in the morning with a surprise."

So Luke was all over the news again. On April 25, he came to Franklin for a hearing on the domestic violence petition. Luke claimed that he did not even own a firearm and that the gunshots LaDonna heard were from him playing a video game. Luke was found guilty. After the hearing, Luke was charged with third-degree terroristic threatening, arrested, and taken to jail. This time, however, he was granted bail. His mother posted a sum of ten thousand dollars, and within hours Luke was freed.

When Luke pleaded not guilty at his arraignment, there was something of a reunion in the courtroom. Not far from Donna Dugas in the audience were Virginia, Barbie, and Lisa, who wordlessly sat exchanging glares with her.

On January 25, 2008, Bruce Dugas was found in his burning Mercedes at a rest stop outside of Bowling Green. He died from smoke inhalation and acute thermal injury. Although the circumstances were mysterious, his death was ruled accidental. Preliminary toxicology reports indicated that he was possibly under the influence of intoxicants. (Bruce had been charged with driving under the influence in 2007 after he ran into a parked semitrailer.) Bruce Dugas's death sparked innuendo that his stepson had something to do with it. Luke, however, was in Texas at the time.

"It's like there's a dark cloud hanging over everyone involved in this," says Donna Dugas.

Late in the summer of 2008, tragedy would again strike. One morning, Barbie White left the home she shared with her family to take her baby to the doctor. When Barbie returned home that afternoon, her mother, Virginia White, was dead. White had overdosed on sleeping pills. Her death was ruled accidental.

Only freshman girls live in Hugh Poland Hall now. The hallways fill each fall with the laughter of a new class ready to embark on a year of self-discovery. Security is particularly tight compared to what it had been in 2003. The RAs instruct their students to inform them if they notice anyone going near the supply closet on the second floor. In a previous incarnation it was room 214.

TIME LINE MAY 4, 2003

Approximately 12 AM
Katie Autry and Danica Jackson arrive at the Pike fraternity party.

Approximately 12:45 AM
Lucas Goodrum, Stephen Soules, Damian Secrest, and Brian Moon arrive at the Pike party. Soules stays in the truck.

Approximately 12:58 AM
Stephen Soules calls Brian Richey asking for a ride.

Approximately 1:13 AM
Stephen Soules calls Richey again. Richey doesn't pick up the call.

Approximately 1:30–2 AM
Katie Autry leaves Pike party with Ryan "Possum" Payne and Stephen Soules.

Approximately 2 AM
Lucas Goodrum, Moon, and Secrest leave the Pike party and walk to Bemis Lawrence Hall.

Approximately 2:04 AM
Moon calls Payne's cell reminding him to pick up Goodrum from Bemis Lawrence Hall.

Approximately 2:15 AM
Moon and Secrest sign in to Bemis Lawrence Hall. Goodrum doesn't sign log and sits on couch in the lobby.

Approximately 2:16 AM
Moon phones Payne again and requests he come pick up Goodrum (cell records).

Approximately 2:25 AM
Payne picks up Goodrum and drives him to Southern Lanes bowling alley.

Approximately 2:26 AM
Danica Jackson calls to check in on her roommate Katie Autry. Jackson also speaks to Stephen Soules.

Approximately 2:50–3 AM
Payne returns to his dorm, Bemis Lawrence Hall.

Approximately 3:10 AM
Goodrum arrives at his father's house according to his father and stepmother, Mike and Judy Goodrum.

Approximately 4:08 AM
Fire alarm sounds at Hugh Poland Hall.

Approximately 4:10 AM
WKU police officer Raphael Casas arrives
on scene and observes smoke in room 214
but is ordered not to enter.

Approximately 4:10–4:12 AM
Sprinkler is activated in room 214.

Approximately 4:14 AM
Bowling Green Fire Department arrives at
Poland Hall.

Approximately 4:27 AM
Katie Autry is discovered in her dorm room
and taken out of the building.

Approximately 4:38 AM
EMS arrive at Poland Hall.

Approximately 4:45 AM
Sprinkler is turned off in room 214.

Approximately 4:50 AM
Katie Autry arrives at Medical Center in
Bowling Green.

Approximately 5:52 AM
Katie Autry taken to burn unit at
Nashville's Vanderbilt University Hospital
via helicopter. She dies on May 7.

ACKNOWLEDGMENTS

Sincere gratitude to all those interviewed.

Special thanks to my resolute editor, Amber Qureshi, and agent, Byrd Leavell.

Reporting and research assistance by Miriam Gross, Kate Hammer, and Cara Tabachnik. Original photography by Marcus Mam and photo research by Lisa Corson are deeply appreciated.

Many thanks for support to Aunt Penny Adams, Adam Baran, Jack Caton, Tara Giannone, Robert Johnston, Angela Kelley, Dan Kellum, Chan Marshall, Tom Masters, Scott Nguyen, Mel Ottenberg, Jaime Perlman, and the Van Meters: Chip, Mary, and Beth McGee.